# Diary of a Hoarder's Daughter

by
Izabelle Winter

# Dedication

This book is dedicated to my mum who suffered
with suspected Alzheimer's disease and passed
away aged 59. This is her story too: sadly, one she
will never be able to tell.

# Acknowledgements

To all my friends and family who hid their shock and got stuck in to help me out; Jackie and Mark, Jane, Andrea, Emma, Anita, Rhian, Cath, Adam and Matthew. Also to friends and family who offered moral support from afar; especially Tanith and Jenny who checked on me daily and sent chocolate.
Thank you. I am eternally grateful.

Also thanks to Jenny and Rob for help and encouragement with this book and for help and honest opinions with editing.

Squidgy hugs to Kieran, Izzy, Cassie and Ian ~ for not complaining too much during the time I was climbing the mountain ~ and writing the book.

# Introduction

Dad was in his own personal paradise ~ his garden. Aged 82 he'd never been one to follow traditional retirement pursuits and on this warm summer's day he was fifteen feet up a ladder which was resting against a large tree.

Dad being up a ladder wasn't unusual; he'd always been one of life's eccentrics. He dearly loved his huge garden and was very much a hands-on man. Most days regardless of the weather he spent hours cutting hedges, weeding, digging, chopping, pruning, mowing and tending. As a result, his lawn was bowling-green smooth, flowers bloomed in carefully weeded beds, and soft fruit hung heavily on the carefully tended bushes.

Since mum passed away nineteen years earlier, he'd whiled away even more hours tending his plants. The neighbours looked at his garden, he was sure, in awe and wonder ~ as of course they should ~ he'd spent many hours getting it just right.

On this particular day even the birds were singing. Life was good. He looked up into the canopy of the tree and considered his next step: it wouldn't need much taken off; unlike the huge elm he'd pruned that morning.

Without warning he began to feel a little odd. He looked away hoping the slightly woozy feeling would subside: it didn't. He closed his eyes, attempting to regain his balance but it was too late…

My brother Ant, who had been holding the ladder, recalled, "There was a loud thud and he was out cold, on the grass." The ladder remained against the tree; it appeared Dad had simply fallen off.

Ant was stricken by panic and fetched a neighbour, who arrived still in wellies, straight from his garden. The neighbour realised nobody had yet called for help and offered to call an ambulance from the house phone.

'No,' screamed poor Ant, almost beside himself with panic ~ 'you can't go in the house!'

It was too late; the neighbour had opened the door: The sight which met him stopped him dead in his tracks.

Despite Dad's garden being immaculate, the house was entirely at the other end of the spectrum. Every room, every surface, every cupboard, every shelf, every single space was filled with stuff, so much stuff that it was impossible to move freely in any of the rooms. Floor to ceiling stuff: all kinds of stuff, with little walkways from room to room, too narrow for one person to pass another. None of the doors would open properly because of all the stuff behind and in front of them. The front door opened barely enough to let someone in ~ and then only if they walked sideways.

And now the neighbour knew.

When I arrived the neighbour was rather pale and looking a little shocked ~ I assumed due to Dad's accident; apparently not.

'I ~ er ~ I think he may have injured his back' said the neighbour.

'Oh Hell!' I said.

'How on earth will he cope with the house ~ with the house ~ *like that?*'

I realised with horror that not only had the neighbour seen inside the house but also that he was right and the house as it was, was no place for someone with an injured back. Gradually a little feeling like a gremlin started in my toes and rapidly spread until I was filled with horror. This house – my nightmare, would have to be dealt with. Just as the fire of my thoughts subsided it rose again. The *only* people who could possibly deal with it were me and Ant. We both had jobs and I had three young children and this would take *far* more time than either of us had. That wasn't the point though it was going to have to be done.

While Dad lay in his hospital bed ordering people about and demanding his immediate release, I struggled to grasp the magnitude of the task I had been saddled with: Unless the state of the house changed drastically, his demands to be allowed home would be refused. Ant worked five days a week and had some learning disabilities making it difficult for him to make decisions and take the initiative. He was also somewhat intimidated by Dad and extremely reluctant to do anything which may have resulted in him getting shouted at. This was now my personal Everest and I had no choice but to climb it. Alone…

~

This book is a true account and details my own incredible journey, by the end of it I would have learned so much about not only my father, but about my late mother ~ and also about myself.

According to statistics, there were an estimated six million hoarders in America in 2012, and it is a proportionately similar story in the UK. Apparently five per cent of people in the UK and USA are affected by Hoarding. It's a very common issue, and if this book helps even one person climb their own personal mountain, then my efforts will all have been worthwhile.

# Chapter 1

I sat at my desk in work staring out of the window, wishing I were somewhere more exciting. The phone lines were quiet ~ people clearly had better things to do on such a lovely Sunday evening than phone a helpline. Counting down the minutes to my evening break, 'Let Me Entertain You' blared from my phone at the bottom of my bag. Mobiles are banned in work for security reasons and once again I had forgotten to mute mine. I grabbed the singing bag and fumbled about for the offending phone to silence it before I got glared at by one of the floor managers.

A sneaky peek revealed it was from home. There was also a text "Call home urgent". Hell! What had the kids done now? I nipped out and rang home. My husband told me, in a 'Guess what he's done this time!' manner that my dad had fallen off a ladder in his garden and was currently flat on his back on the grass, dazed and confused.

My brother Ant, who suffered with learning difficulties, was having a panic attack, because he had no idea what to do. He'd called my husband, who called me at work. With the implications of the situation running through my head, I panicked too, running out of work like a headless chicken.

Dad had come round after his fall gurgling and disorientated, with no idea where he was. The first thing he did, while he was still flat on the ground, was instruct Ant to call a chap at his church to say he didn't think he'd be able to read the lesson that night. Next he told him to fetch the retired GP living in the next street. Ant had done both things before he thought to call me. The GP was out, although his son said he'd pass the message on. The chap at the church had sighed and said he'd find someone else to read the lesson. Clearly neither had realised the severity of the situation or that Dad was still lying on the grass. It was at this point that Ant called my house and my husband called me. Nobody had yet thought to call an ambulance.

I rang Ant from work to say I was on my way and try to get some idea of what had happened. Ant was mid panic-attack and didn't want to call an ambulance as he said he didn't know what to say. I told him to get a neighbour fast and I'd be there as soon as I could.

The neighbour came right round ~ when he realised the situation and that Ant had not called an ambulance he said he would call one and headed for the back door of the house asking where the phone was. Poor Ant – as if he hadn't already been panicking enough. The neighbour opened the door and stopped dead. It was at this point that I arrived on the scene and quickly called 999 on my mobile. I'm not sure if the neighbour was more shocked at the state of the house or my dad falling fifteen feet from a ladder.

The ambulance arrived quickly after I called them and following a brief assessment they whisked him off to the hospital on a spinal-board.

Until those x-rays were assessed nothing could be ruled out and a nasty fall from fifteen feet at his age was likely to be catastrophic. How would he manage with his house the way it was? It was difficult enough to move around it already without being physically impaired. What if he couldn't walk? I was going to have to ensure he could move safely around his house when and if he ever came home. This meant, of course, that the house would have to be tidied at least, if only to prevent him slipping on the loose papers all over the floor.

If a health professional visited the house ~ as they would surely have to following his injury – would they have had the authority to condemn it as being unsafe for him to live in? What if they said he couldn't live at home until it was clear? That was a worst case scenario at that point but the horrible thought invaded my mind and stuck there.

Thoughts went round and round in my head all night. I couldn't sleep. What if he wasn't allowed home? What if he'd broken his back? What if he had to use a wheelchair? The tiny walkways wouldn't possibly allow for a wheelchair. What if the damage turned out to be permanent? What if he could never walk again? Who'd look after him?

I concluded that whatever the outcome of the x-rays, the house as it was would not be a safe environment for him to return to. If a healthcare professional saw the state of it all hell would break loose. Where on earth could he live if not at home?

Whatever happened, that house was going to have to be tidied and the sooner it was done, the better. I estimated it would take years to put right but I didn't have years. It needed to be done in days, and not only that, I was the only one who could do the job, because I was the only one who recognized the importance of ensuring that nothing got thrown out that he might need, want or miss! Twenty-nine years' experience of living in that house had taught me that there may have been a share certificate or two inside any one of those hundreds of newspapers, or a £20 note scrunched up inside a carrier bag. There could have been a mint Penny Black stamp in a plastic wallet put inside an old book to keep it flat and safe. My birth certificate could have been between the leaves of one of those magazines on the table. That shoebox full of papers and old philatelic magazines dated 1979 might be hiding precious family photographs.

No one else on the planet would understand the situation as well as I did, and the idea of the irreparable damage a *man with a van* might do to the house and to Dad's mental state didn't bear thinking about.

I steeled myself to do this alone. It had to be done, no question. The mountain had to be climbed and the sooner the better.

From outside, Dad's house always looked gorgeous: it was a three bedroom 'Dormer' style detached house with the front garden full of flowers and neat shrubs. The large lawn at the back he kept well mown and in summer, fruit bushes were heavy with juicy red and black-currants. Gooseberry bushes grew in the far corner between a large pear tree and two apple trees and regimented rows of runner beans and peas climbed tidily up their symmetrical frames. His rhubarb was legendary and he often sold some to help the local church.

Inside the house, however, things could not have been more different. Dad's hoarding habit filled, floor to ceiling, every room, every space, every cupboard and every walkway. Even the kitchen, the bathroom and the stairs were full of junk. The poor floorboards groaned with the weight of it all.

If a person needed to enter an occupied room, the first person would have to leave to let the second person in. All the doors were wedged permanently open. Towering piles of junk five feet high regularly fell over and were left where they fell.

If the phone rang one faced an obstacle course the Krypton Factor would have been proud of. The bathroom held a pile of newspapers dating from 1987. I couldn't understand how anyone could have looked at those papers every day for twenty-six years and not had the urge to move them.

The Christmas lights were permanently on the wall because they couldn't be reached to take them down; they just got switched on at Christmas. Christmas cards were also a permanent feature, many of those hanging from the string over the fireplace were sent by people who'd been resting in their graves for at least ten years.

When I was young it was normal to have to clear a three foot square patch in the living room for the tree each year.

I felt as if I was at Everest base camp, all alone, wearing just flip-flops and a woolly hat. I was totally unprepared for the nightmare I faced; totally terrified by it and afraid I'd fall on the way up the mountain. I just wanted to go home and hide.

Somehow I had to find the strength to sort this mess out. I still had no idea what state Dad was going to be in long term. I knew that sorting out the house would be difficult enough, but it would be a hundred times worse if he were in the house watching me. I had to do it while he was still in the hospital and I had no idea how much time I had before they released him – and when they did, I wondered if he would ever be able to walk again. From the way the hospital staff had been talking I knew his condition was serious.

I had to start the task as soon as possible but my kids aged eight and ten were on their school summer holiday and we were due to go on a family caravanning holiday three weeks later. Added to family concerns, I was working twenty-five hours a week and had intended to enrol on the second year of a three year carpentry course the following month. How the hell was I going to find the time? Whatever happened – I was going to *have* to find the time.

I drove to his house and let myself in. For the first time in years I was alone with the hoard, trying to get my head around it. I knew I had to forge a plan. The mess wasn't a shock ~ I already knew how he lived. Whenever I went there I got a headache after the first five minutes due to the visual chaos assaulting my eyes. My brain couldn't make sense of it all and I usually had to leave as soon as it was politely possible. The first sneeze was the cue that my allergies were kicking in and it was time to get out. If Dad was there when I called, we'd go into the garden to talk and if it was raining we'd talk in my car. If the kids were with me, we'd still go into the garden or in my car. His house was not the kind of place kids could go.

I had tried to tidy parts of his house on a previous occasion. Once, when he was on holiday, I managed to fill sixteen bin bags full of junk over two weeks and made sure they went to the tip. He never even noticed the difference when he came home and had filled the space with more stuff within a few weeks. I spent a week on asthma steroids due to the effect the dust had on my lungs.

I tried to accept Dad lived in his own house in his own mess. If that was how he wanted to live then who was I to stop him? He always appeared happy enough and the mess didn't appear to bother him.

It certainly bothered me, so I never went there unless I had to. Dad described it as "organised chaos" and pretended to know where everything was. Except, of course, in reality he didn't. He thought he knew where he had seen something last, but this may have been years earlier, so whatever it was had almost certainly been buried by a few more years' worth of layers of stuff.

He'd buy more stuff because he'd lost the original purchases, for instance, shoes and green shirts... He often bought shoes and a shirt in the January sales; he'd take them home and put them, still in their bags, on the top of a pile. After a few weeks or months he'd put more stuff on top until the bag was buried and he forgot it was there. The following year he'd go to the sales and buy more shoes and shirts. I'm sure you get the picture. There were layers of January sales in the hoard and it was almost possible to identify the year of a particular layer by looking at the collar or shoe styles... The lower layers became almost fossilised.

Moving round the house was impossible to accomplish without stepping on something, tripping over something, knocking something over or having to contort one's body to get past. Almost every time I visited he was in his garden, spring, summer, autumn or winter. Dad spent a lot of time in his garden; far more time than anyone else I've ever known. He spent more time in the garden than he did in the house.

In the rear garden grew an evergreen tree that had once grown outside his brother's front door. It was supposed to be a miniature but after five years or so it got too big so Dad took it and planted it in his own garden. Forty or so years later the "miniature" tree was taller than the house and swayed alarmingly when the wind blew. This was the tree the ladder was against when he fell off it.

The ladder still leaned against the tree when I went round the day after the accident to assess what I needed to do. I took it down, summoned my courage, and went into the house.

As I opened the door I was overwhelmed by the musty smell and the most enormous mess I'd ever seen. Looking at it from the point of view of *dealing* with it was entirely different from attempting to ignore it on a social visit. I stood, alone, at the front door and just stared. Where the hell was I supposed to start? I was totally unprepared. I sat on the front step and howled and howled and howled. Defeated for the day, I went home.

~

The hospital rang that evening and told me that Dad had broken his back and his collar bone. They were being typically noncommittal and said he'd be there for quite a while.

# Chapter 2

I hadn't been in the house alone in about twenty years and this was the first time I'd had the opportunity to fully absorb the current state of it. I'd never envisaged having to tidy this mess by myself. I'd often idly wondered what would happen when the inevitable occurred – but in that scenario there were many, many skips! Never in my wildest nightmares did I ever imagine having to *tidy* it. Throwing out junk was easy, but to tidy was entirely different. Sorting what was important in someone else's eyes and knowing they'd return to judge was a nightmare in the making.

I decided to start in the porch area behind the front door so the door could be properly opened, this would enable me to bring stuff outside. The porch was about three feet by seven feet and from it I sorted: a few rubber overshoes, three sandals ~ all unmatched, mountains of junk mail, a local free newspaper from about 1987, various electrical components, lots of free shampoo sachets, hairy string, a wall mountable flowerpot, twelve copies of the Radio Times ~ all 13th July 2002, three tins of soup dated 2006, an empty cereal box, a shoe brush, an entire carton of six bottles of posh wine, two woolly hats, a bag of corks, a still wrapped child's t-shirt, age six to twelve months, three pine cones, a reel of wire, a box of three electrical plugs, lots of free newspapers, an unidentifiable sticky substance in a tin, a dusty sock and seven Scout-post Christmas cards, unopened, which judging from the stamps were at least six years old.

Under all this junk was a coffee table with the skinniest legs I'd ever seen which had been wilting under the weight all of this stuff for a good twenty to thirty years. Next to and underneath the table were 27 bottles of wine old and new, three commercial lighting units, three boxes of bits and a carrier bag full of pieces of a broken wing mirror from his Ford Focus which was smashed off three years previously and replaced a month later. There were magazines and catalogues from 1982, newspapers from 1996, junk mail and a brand new Readers Digest book *"Spot's first Christmas"* aimed at two to three year olds which I assume he bought for my kids now aged eight and ten.

Dumped in the corner was an old wooden-case record player. This had been salvaged from a skip outside a neighbour's house following his death in 2002. Under that were twelve tins of spaghetti, eighteen tins of soup, a big bag of garden fertiliser, a roll of electrical earth wire, half a bicycle mudguard, an old inner tube and a brand new, still packaged *"My Little Pony"* pencil case, eraser, pencil and key ring. In another box were four pairs of new garden clogs. Asked later why he'd bought four pairs he said he'd bought them online and needed to buy enough pairs to make the postage viable. There were two extension leads, several bits of wood, a paperback book, seven unworn leather sandals from Spain, hundreds of perished rubber bands, some rusty keys, three boxes with bits of wood in, an old black telephone, a brand new book of stamps including ½p values, an electrical catalogue from 1998, a pot of plastic flowers, three rusty dog leads, a cracked barometer and an old, but unused photo album. That's just what I can remember.

It took five hours, sorting that porch. It all came out and filled the thirteen large steps leading up to the house. Most of it went back in. The porch still looked terrible and after five hours of non-stop hard labour all I had to show for it was a front door that could now be opened. The rest of the house remained untouched. This was going to take forever.

There were four large bags of recycling and two bags of rubbish which I managed to persuade his neighbours to put in their bins. Dad had filled his own two huge bins with small bits of wood.

I felt smelly, dirty and itchy. My hair was full of dust, my nose was runny, my eyes were dry and I desperately needed a bath, but at least I felt I'd achieved something. I had dented the mountain.

~

The following day I went to the bank to pay a bill for Dad before going to visit him in the hospital. I told him I'd paid his bill in cash. Nevertheless he spent the next thirty minutes telling me, in great detail, how to pay a bill for him by cheque. He got very irritated that I would not listen to him and learn, followed by further abuse for not going to *his* branch as apparently they knew him in there so they could have sorted the bill for him. I tactfully explained that as a fully functioning adult I was familiar with cheques and indeed had even had my own cheque account for many years. I also reminded him I had actually worked for a bank for eleven years.

I carefully and patiently explained that, due to the Data Protection Act and indeed customer security, which was for his own protection, a letter would not suffice. I reiterated that I had *already* paid his bill with my own cash and he could pay me back with a cheque.

Despite all this he exclaimed; "To hell with the bloody Data Protection Act; this bill needs to be paid". Ten minutes later I was wondering whether hurling myself out of the sixth floor hospital window would have made him listen to me. Perhaps that was a bit extreme but I wasn't convinced even that would work.

He was extremely irritated that I wasn't listening to him. Why hadn't I taken my three small children to a bank a fifteen minute car journey away to hand in a letter I knew they wouldn't accept despite the fact *they knew him in there*? How inconsiderate it was of me to pay for his bill with *my* cash as then he had to fill in a cheque to repay me, except I had already filled it in to save time ~

17

he just had to sign it. How bloody incompetent I clearly was because the banks no longer worked on trust.

He said, in front of me, to Ant: "Your sister can be quite nice when she's not in a bad mood."

Through gritted teeth I pointed out I'd spent *five hours* clearing just his porch that day so that he could come home.

He replied, "Heaven only knows what's been thrown out!"

Dad had written a list of things for me to bring to the hospital for him. I had to go to his house *again* to get these. I didn't expect thanks, of course. However he acted as if I should feel it was the highlight of *my* day when I visited him. The fact I had eight year old twin daughters and a ten year old son, all on holiday from school didn't figure in his calculations, and neither did the fact that I worked four nights a week from 3:30 until 9:30 so had to visit the hospital before my shift on the days I worked.

He said, 'You can bring my radio when you come tomorrow.' Without asking whether I'd be able to come or even if I'd mind coming!

'Tomorrow I'll be in to visit between two and three, Dad because I'm working.'

'When do you finish work?' he said, ignoring me.

'Usual time Dad, nine thirty, so I'll be in between two and three. I've worked the same hours for the past year.'

'Oh that's *far* too late! You can't come then, it's too late!'

'No Dad. That's why I'm coming in between two and three.'

'What time do you start?'

'Usual time Dad three thirty, same time I always start, so I'll come between two and three.'

'Well then, you can come before that.' he said, as if he'd just sorted out the problem.

He did have a hearing aid once but he lost it in about 1996. No surprise there really. There was never any acknowledgement that it may have been *him* who had the hearing issue ~ he acted more like it was *me* who had a speech impediment! Either this, or as I suspected, he believed I simply had nothing of any intelligence or importance to say.

When I arrived home, after dropping Ant back to the house, I noticed the old record player in my car that had been retrieved from the skip after his neighbour had died. I'd intended to take it to the recycling centre the next day. I was *so* wound up I *accidentally* dropped it getting it out of the car. Something snapped in my head at that point, the red mist descended and I proceeded to kick it to death. I kicked it right down the street and then back up again. Then I scraped all fifty-three pieces off the road, threw them across my garden then stamped on them. I was a bit irrational by then, I admit and was in a bit of a frenzy. Finally I picked up the battered carcass and threw it onto the patio. I felt marginally better. My neighbours may have been a little concerned though. I hoped nobody had seen me!

# Chapter 3

I didn't sleep too well that night. I don't often get headaches but the stress was getting to me and after tossing and turning half the night I decided to take a headache tablet. With hindsight that wasn't wise, because I dreamed of mountains of *stuff* coming to get me and me not being able to escape. Finally I dreamed that I was trying to kill something ~ or someone. When I woke up my eye hurt and when I looked in the mirror it looked as if I had been fighting ~ I'd attacked myself. I had a black eye and I'd evidently dug my nails into my own nose. The hoard was driving me insane...

~

The next day my elderly neighbour approached me, somewhat cautiously, as I loaded the kids into the car. She enquired about my wellbeing. I thought this was a little strange but instinct told me it was probably best to tell her what she wanted to hear.

'I'm fine, thanks,' ~ I even managed a cheery smile ~ it was probably more of a grimace, but the thought was there.

'Oh,' she said, digging into her pocket, 'only, I found this by your car and thought you may need it.' She produced the arm from the record player I'd murdered the previous day.

'Oh, er, thank you!' I said, smiling sweetly.

She stared at me. 'Are you *sure* you're OK?'

'Oh, hahaha!' I laughed, somewhat unconvincingly, realising she must have seen the record player incident. She clearly now thought I was a closet axe murderer. 'The record player was too big to fit in my car so I had to break it up. The boot's teeny weeny ~ look.' My voice trailed off. I knew what she was thinking.

'OK', she said, rather nervously, 'Well, if you need anything dear...' She took several steps backwards before walking briskly back to the safety of her house. I'm sure I heard her bolt the door behind her.

I took the kids with me to the mountain because their dad was working. I'd decided to sort the back of the house this time. Perhaps this was a tactic to delay actually going inside ~ one day the porch, the next outside the back of the house. I convinced myself I was being methodical. The house had an overhanging shelter immediately outside the back door. I needed this space clear so I could put stuff there where it wouldn't get wet. First, I phoned the council to collect the two damp, mouldy armchairs which had been outside the patio doors for more than seven years. Once these were gone the doors could be opened.

I started clearing and within two minutes the kids, all totally bored, had disappeared. Luckily the huge garden gave them space to play. I was sure they'd be fine.

From outside the back door I collected bags of leaves, twigs, bits of plastic, old plant pots, yoghurt pots, string, carrier bags, my old school shoe from when I was six and half a welly. There were also some bits which I was afraid might be pieces of asbestos roof that had been replaced many years before. I sealed them in a rubble sack.

An hour or so later the kids were so bored they were running riot and I couldn't carry on working. I had to call it a day and I took them home, stopping for a walk around the park on the way.

I vowed to do better the following day. I already felt I couldn't face any more, especially with the kids around. I was torn. I felt guilty: I should have been doing what good mothers should do in school holidays and taking the kids to the park or the beach or just spending time with them. I had a bit of a howl. Would it ever get done? I hadn't even managed to get properly started.

When I went to see Dad later that day I was determined to broach the subject of the clear-out. At that point he still hadn't agreed that I should do it. He said he realised it probably should be done and that one of his worst nightmares was just such a scenario ~ not having had time to clear up and then something happening. I had to bite my lip. I didn't mention that climbing up a ladder into a tree possibly hadn't been one of his better ideas either and may well have contributed to his worst nightmare coming true. However, I felt that, unfairly, this particular nightmare was all mine.

I don't think that at that point he'd linked the two factors ~ his back was broken and his house had to be tidied. I didn't push it because it seemed a bit uncaring to be talking about such a sore subject that was frankly, in his mind at least, irrelevant.

The scale of the clear-up was not the only thing which worried me. I've suffered from chronic asthma since I was three years old and was hospitalised after my first attack, since then I've spent many more occasions in hospital for the same reason. Dad's house was clearly not the best place for an asthmatic.

Intriguingly, since I moved out in 1994 I've only had two asthma attacks, both following visits to people who owned animals. I've always been allergic to animal fur and could never go into friends' houses if they had a cat or dog. This made socialising difficult ~ most of my friends had one of the two. I recall a friend organising a *Titanic* film night at her house. Her neighbour's cat had been sitting on her couch and within ten minutes of arriving I was sneezing, wheezing and had puffy red itchy eyes. I had to leave her house before *Titanic* even left the dock.

My allergies were far more severe than just a few sneezes. A typical allergic reaction started with itchy eyes and sniffles, followed by a full blown asthma attack. The most extreme reaction to an animal resulted in me spending five days on a life support machine after suffering a respiratory arrest aged 22. Since then I don't risk entering a house with a resident furry animal. Banishing the animal to the garden doesn't help. Moving the animal to the neighbour's house for the day, vacuuming and damp dusting the whole house doesn't help, either. The allergen comes from the skin, the fur and the saliva of the animal. I can't go to a friend's house for coffee. I can't call for a friend before a night out unless I sit in the car and wait which makes me appear unsociable. If my mad cat lady colleague sits in the desk next to me at work, I struggle to breathe. I am unable to go to certain pubs for a meal with my friends because of a resident dog.

In one former job a colleague had an eyesight problem which got progressively worse until she eventually required a guide dog. She brought the dog to the office and I suffered so much I left the job. I didn't feel able to complain ~ that would have hurt her feelings. It didn't help that another colleague said she was also allergic to animals, yet she owned three cats! She just took an antihistamine tablet every day which controlled her mild allergy. My allergies aren't mild, and it's difficult to explain about them without sounding like a major hypochondriac. Antihistamine, to me, is like taking aspirin before a leg amputation. Most of the time I deal with them by avoiding places likely to set me off. I've become very upfront and matter of fact about it although my friends describe me jokingly as *High Maintenance.*

Although fur is the worst allergen for me, dust, mould and damp also affect me. My doctor has told me that all the asthma attacks I had when I was younger had damaged my lungs. I can't afford to take risks with my health any more.

Dad's house has been more or less off limits to me for years. Once I'd moved out I had absolutely no plans to ever go back. I was able to go to the garden for visits but not inside the house. I didn't want to go in, not only because of the dust ~ but the visual chaos played havoc with my brain. Dad also had a miniature poodle called Tyson. I've been told so many times by well-meaning friends that poodles are OK for allergy sufferers. They are undoubtedly better but not allergy free. I tried looking after Tyson once when Dad went on holiday. He was bathed and groomed before the visit but within a day I was at the hospital again on a nebuliser and Tyson had to go to the kennels.

Now I was facing a total nightmare: I had to enter the house to sort out the mess and it would take a long time. There was simply nobody else who could do it. My friends had offered their help, but I was pretty sure none of them knew Dad was a hoarder, and if they did know, they had no idea of the scale of it. This was going to be a shock. It never came up in normal conversation ~ and it wasn't anything I ever chose to share with people. I may have mentioned that Dad was a dreadful hoarder, but the response was always something like, "Oh God, yes, I know that feeling! You can't move in my garage!", or, "Yes I know. I'm dreadfully messy too! You should just see my attic." They simply had *no idea*.

Dad's garage was crammed full, as were the front room, the living room, the three bedrooms, the bathroom, the kitchen, the stairs, the landing and the hallway. The shed was also full to bursting, and the coal house and greenhouse too. But at least after my earlier efforts it was possible to go in through the front door and the porch without having to walk sideways!

Word got out that Dad was in hospital and people started calling round to his house with get well cards. I had to invite them inside because I had no time to stop and chat ~ and if these people were truly his friends then perhaps they might have offered help.

Most of the neighbours knew me from my childhood and were aware there was a clutter issue, they could see it through the front windows, but I don't think any of them realised the full extent of it. Two of them came over to bring me a mug of coffee and some homemade cake. They offered space in their bins, assuming Dad's bin would be full. They were right; although why Dad had filled both bins with bits of wood I have no idea. The neighbours were all very sympathetic and they offered green bags, black bags, dustpan and brush and a vacuum cleaner. Dad had three vacuum cleaners ~ all of which had become buried under the clutter years before and hadn't been seen since.

Looking at the house from outside, nothing looked wrong. All the neighbours tried to hide their shock when they saw the inside. I wasn't shocked ~ I grew up in that house although it was never quite as bad then.

I enjoyed my chats with the neighbours, who all talked about my mum, saying how fondly they remembered her. A kind and thoughtful lady, they said, with a very kind heart, always willing to help, loved by the neighbourhood kids, hardworking, softly spoken, patient and kind. They all said how tragic it was that she went the way she did and how it upset them all on a personal level to see the terrible transformation from Mum as we all knew her to an empty, confused, angry, upset and frightened individual. Every single one of them said it was terrible to see her have the breakdown.

The Breakdown! As far as I was aware it had been Alzheimer's disease that had taken Mum at such an early age. Dad said so. Ant and I were teenagers when she first became ill. I was 15 and Ant 14, and at that age we accepted what we were told and believed the adults around us. Mum was very upset when the word *Alzheimer's* was used around her. She absolutely refused to accept it as a diagnosis. The medical profession said it could never be 100% diagnosed without a post mortem brain autopsy. It was very rare, they said, in someone so young. Mum was 47 when things appeared to be not quite right. Early onset Alzheimer's, they said, tended to run in families. There was no history of it in our family.

'Your poor mother,' one neighbour said, 'in the beginning she'd visit our house almost every week bringing bags of rubbish to put in our bin. We had no idea the house was like this because she always came to us. We never went to her. Now I can understand why.'

Another neighbour told me, 'Your poor mother used to come to our house with bags of rubbish. She said your father would never throw them away. We considered it to be just one of those things. Now I can understand what she meant. She used to sit on my sofa and pour her heart out, bless her. She used to get so frustrated with him that she was not able to do anything or have a nice safe and tidy house for you and your brother because of the amount of stuff he kept. She couldn't even get her sewing machine out to do something quick because she'd have to fight with the junk on the table. I don't know how she managed to have enough space to do her school and university work. She wasn't even able to clear the table for dinner because he would always have his stuff on it. It was terrible, you know. We felt so powerless to do anything for her. Of course she was always welcome for coffee but you know we could all see the change in her. I could see she was having a breakdown.'

Yet another neighbour expressed horror at the state of the place. 'Oh my goodness' she said, 'when your mother used to describe the place of course we didn't believe her ~ we thought it was the illness talking, but...' (at this point the neighbour became tearful) 'we were so close in this street ~ all us ladies ~ we all had our children at around the same time. We could all see she had a lot on her plate with you and your brother and a full time teaching job and studying for her Open University Degree at the same time. Of course you with all your health problems and your brother having his disability ~ and ~ and of course *this*.' She gestured to the mess. 'If it were my house I would have lost it a long time before she did. She was so very patient with him. Of course you and your brother were only young – you never knew the half of it.'

I said I'd always accepted what I had been told, that it was Alzheimer's.

'Oh no!' she said firmly ~ but then appeared to change her mind, 'but of course you were just a kid then.'

These neighbours' visits were extremely enlightening. I was very grateful for their company and of course the coffee and cakes. It was the first opportunity I'd ever really had to speak with the neighbours on an adult level. These ladies my mum had known so well as close friends, confidantes and shoulders to cry on. They had all played a daily part in her life for many years. The street they all lived in was a *cul-de-sac* with no through traffic, the type of place where everyone knew and respected everyone else. They had a babysitting circle, a skill swap rota and all the kids played in the street together in total safety. Mum and Dad moved into the street as newlyweds when the house was built in about 1960. They all had children of about the same age and the neighbours knew Mum right up until she was admitted to the local mental hospital for her own safety. It was almost as if now I was an adult, they believed I deserved to know the truth ~ whatever that was.

Those conversations were real eye openers.

# Chapter 4

Ant found a gammon joint in the fridge that Dad had taken out of the freezer on the day of his unscheduled dismount from the ladder.

'What shall I do with it?' he asked me. I glanced at the date; it was two days old.

'I don't think you should eat it,' I said, 'Dad should've put it in the freezer.'

'He did,' said Ant. 'He took it out last week. Shall I put it back in?'

'NO!' I said, horrified. 'You can't re-freeze it. It'll have to go out.' At this point I noticed it was actually dated two years and two days previously ~ I hadn't looked at the year!

'Do you want it?' he asked.

'Hell no. It'll have to go out.'

'Dad'll go mad.' Poor Ant was getting nervous.

'Well I'm not having it in my freezer or my fridge or even in my bin.'

'We'd better ask Dad.' said Ant, clearly gripped by blind panic at the likely repercussions of throwing a whole joint out and realising the bin men would not be round for it until the following Tuesday.

At the hospital later I told Dad the joint was there and it would have to go out.

He said in horror, 'Oh no! You can't throw it out! It'll be OK if we cook it.' *Seriously*! You couldn't make it up.

I had a quick peek at the oven while I was in the house. It should have been condemned years ago. Greasy black stuff coated the inside, so thick it would have needed chiselling off. I don't think he'd used the oven in a fair while, I certainly hoped he hadn't. It was the same oven which had been in the house since it was built in 1960. He still used the hot plate on top and possibly the grill underneath but I was pretty sure even he wouldn't have attempted to roast anything in it. My mother had been the last person to clean or cook in that oven ~ and she'd died nineteen years ago.

Of the eight days since his fall, I'd visited Dad in hospital on seven of them, and every day the hospital staff, professionally vague, said he'd probably be in for a few more days. I knew he couldn't possibly come home safely with the level of junk in the house. I mentioned this to a nurse, who laughed dismissively and said her house was pretty untidy too. She had no idea.

The enormity of the task was still sinking in. Dad could be a cantankerous old stick at the best of times and I couldn't see him letting me clear anything while he was home. It had been mentioned by various sources that if help was needed the house would need to be assessed and action agreed to by the authorities *before* he was released from hospital as it was almost impossible to get assistance afterwards. He was already talking about coming home.

Dad was obviously aware there was a *mess* in the house which he knew had to be cleared and which, he was always eager to point out, he was *dealing with slowly but surely*. This had been his standard response over the past thirty or so years. Oddly he hadn't thought to mention it to the nurses ~ possibly having lived with it for so long he just didn't see it any more. Over time it had become part of the house itself and more and more *normal*.

I still couldn't think of anybody who'd be able to help me with this massive task. Of my friends who had already offered their help, most of them had never actually seen the house and of those who had, not for twenty years or so. I was the only person who could manage this. I couldn't let any clearance company near the place because this was still his home. The stuff was all his and I had no more right to go into his house and throw out his belongings than I would if I were to go into the house next door and throw out their belongings. At least I had some idea of what *was* rubbish, or more to the point what was definitely *not* rubbish as that was easier to decide.

Most people would view a twenty year old broken record player as junk, pure and simple. However to Dad it was a thing of beauty which could have been lovingly restored. The fact he had seven others in the house, one of which he had acquired from a skip and another he had been given by a neighbour for firewood, was beside the point. He saw potential value in everything. The fact he already had one or even thirty-one others in his house was not a part of his decision making process should an opportunity arise to acquire another. He also had an uncanny ability to know exactly how many of these items he actually had even though he didn't know precisely where they were.

~

I asked the kids if they fancied going to Granddad's house again. Their response was a unanimous and emphatic 'NO'. I couldn't really blame them. They'd been so bored the last time. Their presence was counter-productive as well ~ every five minutes or so I'd hear something somewhere crash and would have to go and investigate.

As the weather was good and I decided to nip out on my motorbike, a Kawasaki EN500, to blow all the cobwebs away and to relieve some built-up stress. I went to the bank for Dad and then over to the mountain to let Tyson out. Being on the bike and dressed in leathers, there was little I could do at base camp other than open the front door and sigh, because I had neither mask nor gloves and no way to take stuff to the skip. I made a half-hearted effort at sorting and managed to fill six black bags to go to the skip the following day.

On the way home some clown thought it would be a good idea to reverse his car out of his driveway without looking ~ just as I was riding past. He stopped suddenly as he saw me at the last minute, by which time I was almost on the opposite side of the road. I put the stand down on the bike and went to have a quick *chat* with him.

In my defence, please bear in mind that I was somewhat stressed. I'd also discovered inner wild homicidal axe-murderer tendencies and was most definitely a woman on a mission. Add this to the fact I had three very bored kids on their school holidays and the result was a ticking time bomb.

The bomb went off.

During our ensuing "chat", I think I questioned this gentleman's ability to drive, parentage, intellectual ability, sexual preferences and down-time activities all at a few decibels louder than usual and with a little bit more animation. I may have even said a naughty word or two.

The poor chap did look somewhat taken aback by my monologue and may have muttered something akin to 'Get a boyfriend love'. I let that one slide.

I felt a lot better afterwards and completed my journey home without further mishap.

# Chapter 5

I contacted a specialist clutter clearing service, partly to test the water and possibly get some advice. They told me their company specialised in sorting and tidying and had vast experience doing similar jobs. Apparently they were highly specialised and they were eager to point out they were very fast. I wasn't convinced fast was best in this case though because fast could not possibly be thorough. When I asked the cost I wasn't prepared for the reply; the cost was £30 to £40 an hour.

Brief calculation 1 x Millennium @ £40 an hour = too much. That was the end of *that* idea.

I was in work that night venting my frustrations to my colleagues when one of them suggested I tried to get a television company involved. There were a fair few hoarding programmes on television at the time such as 'The Hoarder Next Door' and 'Buried Alive' and others besides. There was no way I could see Dad agreeing to that sort of public humiliation; besides, he didn't actually think he had a problem. I could hardly *out* him without his knowledge while he was in hospital. As much as it was tempting to grab at any passing straws, he was still my father and in hospital with a broken back and collarbone ~ how could I add mental stress as well? What sort of daughter would do such a thing? However, I also knew I couldn't possibly do this alone.

It was important to keep reminding myself that the contents of his house didn't belong to me, so I really had no right to throw anything out. On the other hand I had to do *something* to enable him to be able to move around safely. Clearly, drastic action was needed although I was very aware that I couldn't allow anyone else to throw his stuff out.

The TV programmes on hoarding all had different approaches. Some took everything out and put it all in a large building, then walked the hoarder round their belongings so they could see how much stuff they had. The idea appeared to be to kick start them into getting rid of some of it. Other programmes tried to gently talk the hoarder through their belongings one by one with a similar aim. I doubted either of these approaches would have worked in Dad's case.

I knew that the TV programmes' main aim was to provide entertainment and therefore they were likely to twist the issue to make the hoarder look like an idiot. On the plus side they were likely to do it for free.

I thought I'd try mentioning the idea briefly in conversation on my next visit to the hospital.

~

Two of my friends, Anita and Emma had offered their help. They came round early the following day. If they hadn't offered, I probably would have just sat down in the garden and howled.

I'd decided that of all the rooms the kitchen was the best place to start; being the most used room in the house. It was so cluttered that the main table wasn't even visible. It certainly wasn't hygienic. My friends, both down to earth types, were both brave enough to enter the house without full ghost-buster suits, gloves, masks and wellies. They pretended not to be horrified. They brought stuff out to the garden, box by box, where I sorted it.

In the kitchen we found a number of unidentifiable bottles of liquid, about seven pairs of wellies, eight single sandals, bits of string, half an old iron and perished rubber gloves. Astonishingly we found about £60 sterling and 50 in Euros just scrunched up loosely in a margarine tub. There were unopened jam jars from 2006 and biscuits from 2002. A bottle of what appeared to be wine, opened, at a guesstimate, in 1973, was murky with bits in and so went straight down the drain. There were old empty and flattened cereal boxes piled together, empty and washed milk cartons, hundreds of carrier bags, jars, bits of wire, fuses, corks, used stamps, Christmas cards, jar lids, chipped crockery, a plastic dinosaur, a plush koala bear, a few old light bulbs, half plugs and lots of unidentifiable bits. Oddly there were many bottles of cleaning liquids and bleach!

Sixteen recycling bags, three huge council green bins and three council black wheelie bins later we had hit the kitchen quarter-way mark. I was halfway through yet another box when I almost got bitten by something wrapped in tissue paper in a plastic bread bag. On closer inspection it was a pair of Dad's false teeth. I have no idea how long they had been missing or how old they were. They'd disappeared into the ether many years ago. I figured they may be important and thought he would be thrilled that I'd found them, so I wrapped them carefully in some tissue paper and put them aside in a safe place.

Ten minutes later the teeth had gone. I checked the dog ~ not guilty. I looked at the mountain of bags I had just tied up to be recycled. Had I, in the state my head was in, thrown them out by mistake? Oh hell! Like a woman possessed I started looking through everything, all the green bags which were still open and also through the black bags already tied up. I didn't find the teeth nor did I have the time to carry on looking. Time was creeping on and I had to go to work so I stopped looking and continued sorting.

Then, a breakthrough ~ a shriek from inside ~ 'We've found the table!' There was no stopping us. We were making progress.

I was outside fishing through stuff when Anita came out with a £20 note that she'd found folded up, loose in a box. Emma came out with two more, tucked in an envelope. Another was wrapped inside a receipt dated 1996. This demonstrated the reason why I couldn't trust the house-sorting to anyone but me and my close friends.

*Everything*, no matter how small, had to be carefully checked. A further shriek came from inside the kitchen; Ant had finally cleared a space in front of a cupboard and managed to open the door. It appeared the cupboard had been shut since the early 90's as the papers in front of it were dated 1992. He'd found three tins of tomato soup, one of which had evidently exploded at some point. I looked for a date on the antique soup tins ~ for my amusement rather than anything else ~ I couldn't find one, but, interestingly, although unsurprisingly, neither could I find any barcodes.

An interesting black slime had formed on the outside of two of the tins. The smell was *vile*.

Flicking through some more paperwork bound for the bin, I found an unused book of stamps ~ 24 brand new 2nd class stamps and a bag of £1 coins with a few more £5 and £10 notes. I still hadn't found the teeth.

*Sixteen* green bags of recycling, three full black bin bags and lots more odd bits of junk later we decided it was time to wrap up for the day. It had also just started raining and I had to go to work. We put all the stuff back inside and left. I drove home via the recycling centre in time to have a quick shower and a cup of tea.

A short while later I was standing in reception at work, fumbling in my bag for my security pass when I came across the teeth, *in my handbag.* Yuck*!*

# Chapter 6

I was at the mountain by seven the next morning. Our efforts the previous day had made a noticeable difference to the kitchen. Ant had been busy already, emptying cupboards and cleaning twenty years' worth of yellow sticky stuff from the kitchen surfaces. He pointed to 27 tins of spaghetti, soup and baked beans which he had put in the garden and to one in particular which felt "a bit light". On further investigation it was still intact, but appeared to be empty, though covered in a rusty sludge. *Nice*! A similar tin appeared to be hissing and on closer inspection, it really *was* hissing, obviously upset by being disturbed from its rest in the cupboard for twenty years or so. All the tins went straight into the bin.

Outside, I tried to move a tin of paint in order to make more space. The tin came up with the handle but the bottom of the tin had rusted to the ground and stayed put. The whole thing disintegrated and its entire contents, a bagful of little gravel stones, wrapped in a Tesco carrier bag, fell out all over the floor. The bag was still intact. Ecologically, I found it worrying that a Tesco bag had survived where a metal tin did not.

Carrier bags are no longer given away free in Wales for "green" reasons, as they take too many years to disintegrate. I don't know how many years it officially takes a carrier bag to totally break down. In the kitchen there were about six strong reusable carrier bags, themselves stuffed full of 2-300 other carrier bags. When I tried to move them, those at the bottom came out in snow-like flurries. They had disintegrated almost into dust.

That house is an eco-experiment come to life.

The same day we also uncovered eighteen more bottles of wine, three cans of beer dated 2005, about forty tins of soup, spaghetti and baked beans, a whole pile of shop receipts and visa card receipts from the age when you used to have to sign for visa transactions; 97 used stamps, three hundred or so corks from wine bottles, another book from Readers' Digest post-marked fourteen years previously, still in its unopened postage box, three more wellies, five unmatched leather sandals from Benidorm, one plastic frog, a brand new frying pan, half a Henry Hoover, a box of 36 halogen light bulbs, two toasters, a toasted sandwich maker, a yoghurt maker, eight table mats and a new, wrapped set of new-born baby gloves and hat, presumably for one of my three kids. There were bags of unmatched socks, seven more pairs of new gardening gloves, two large jars of coffee dated 2006, three £20 notes tucked inside a receipt, a further book of 24 new second class stamps, lots of papers, brochures and old letters, a Christmas balloon, thirty or so Christmas cards to the family ~ unopened, one from a relative who died in 1997, a jar of old batteries, sixteen chipped mugs and a bathroom tap.

At 3:00 we started to clear up as we needed to visit Dad in the hospital and so stuff had to go back inside overnight in case it rained.

When we got to the hospital at 3:45 Dad was sleeping. I poked him gently.

'Oh,' he said, 'I thought nobody was coming so I decided to take a nap.'

'Well here we are.' I said, trying to act upbeat.

'Yes, I can see that.'

'I've picked up your glasses for you Dad; here they are.' The glasses had taken me two car trips to the optician and a number of telephone calls to get sorted.

'How much were they?' he asked, '£8?'

'Yes'

'£7?'

'£8 Dad.'

'Yes, I said, £8.' Once again I noted the lack of the two little words "thank" and "you".

'Oh yes I meant to say ~ about the car, ~ the MOT is due soon.'

'Dad, do you mean the road tax? That's got four months left. I can get it cashed in for you if you like, before the end of the month.'

'No!' he said. 'The MOT is due in four months but if you take it to the, um to the, um...'

'The DVLA tax office, Dad, but you need a form from the Post Office.'

'NO! *Listen!*' he shouted at me, as if I were rudely interrupting. 'You have to get it done before September or you lose another month on the MOT.'

'It's *tax*, Dad. You mean *tax*. The first of the month is not until next Sunday so we have eight days.'

He shouted over me, 'Ant will have to go to the local Post Office. It has to be done soon. You have to ask them what form you need. What date is it?'

I gave up. I was obviously, yet again, just displaying my inadequacies by not listening to the Maestro who was clearly the *only* one on the planet who had ever heard of the concept of cashing in a tax disc. I was *such* an idiot. Imagine me thinking I knew how to do it and that I could get a form from the Post Office or even download one! Silly me! How could I possibly have known this, being only forty five years old?

I said, 'It's the 25th, Dad,' knowing it was futile to attempt to halt his tirade.

'Right then, so we have until...' counting days in his head... 'Friday, so Ant will have to go to see what he needs to do and let me know or get a form and bring it in to me. Ant, are you in town on Tuesday?'

'Dad,' I almost screamed. 'I will download it, bring it in tomorrow for you to sign and drop it up the DVLA *tomorrow*! Job done.'

'Oh I *wish* you'd listen to me,' he said. 'Ant will see what needs to be done and then I will have to sort it out. Ant can go on the bus on Thursday. Oh, but then we have a Bank Holiday, and you see if you miss the month end which will be um ~ Friday, because, you see it is closed on Saturday ~ then you'll lose a month so it will have to be done this week.'

At this point I had to leave the room before my inner axe murderess surfaced.

As I left I heard him say loudly to Ant, 'I really don't know *what*'s the matter with your sister these days.'

The fact I'd spent fourteen hours over the past two days neck deep in his crap so he could come home, plus visited him both days, and *then* gone to work as well, didn't appear to have registered with him at all.

I remembered the words of one of the neighbours who visited him last week in hospital. 'I was a bit concerned at your father's unfaltering belief in your ability to be in four places simultaneously.'

Turning, I said as calmly and as slowly and clearly as I could, rather like the way one would speak to a small child, 'Dad. Listen to me. I can get a form printed off my computer at home and I will bring it to you in hospital to sign.'

He looked at me as if I were the most obtuse and ungrateful creature on the planet. 'I was only trying to make things easier,' he said in hurt tones.

I wondered again if those sixth floor safety windows would open wide enough for me to squeeze through.

~

I was at base station by 8am the next day, a woman on a mission. I couldn't spend the full day there as I'd promised to take the kids out, to the cinema and various other places. There was only a week left before they went back to school and I felt I'd let them down badly. I hadn't been there for them over the school holidays.

There was still a lot of stuff in the garden from the previous day. Once things had been brought outside to sort it seemed somewhat counter-productive to take them all back in at night when time ran out because then, everything would have to be brought back out again in the morning. Dad had a large shed and a large detached garage but these were both full to bursting with stuff. I moved a pile of logs away from the door so that it was safe to open it and step outside carrying stuff, and as I moved them it became apparent that there was something big underneath. This turned out to be a washing machine.

Why would anyone keep an old, broken, and now rusty washing machine? It had been covered in a tarpaulin and then logs put on top. It must have been outside for at least ten years. I can't imagine something that big, something I'd have to squeeze past daily to get out the door, being in *my* garden for years. I hadn't spotted it before because it was hidden. I rang the council who were booking collection slots for three weeks later.

It appeared that Dad's neighbours had been bringing their scrap wood and old furniture to him for years under the misguided belief that they were doing an old man a favour by providing kindling for his fire. Either that or he had been skip pilfering. He had enough logs to last him a lifetime.

He'd already set his chimney on fire two years before, due to not getting it swept in over twenty years. He told me about this "minor mishap" a few days after the event. The chimney was apparently well ablaze and he'd tried to put it out with buckets of water. He didn't call the fire brigade, he said because he didn't want to have water damage in his house! Wasn't fire damage worse? The truth, I suspect, was he did not want the firemen to condemn the house and to tell him off. All the plaster on the bedroom wall where the chimney was, remained cracked. I doubted the chimney had been swept since the fire, either!

In my quest to get more space outside where I could store stuff removed from inside, I decided to clear the single storey, single layer brick coal-house. It was about 4ft x 9ft, attached to the outside of the house. When I was small it was used to store coal and wood for the fire. For the previous twenty or so years it had been full of plastic sacks, cardboard, bits of wood and junk. Had anyone dared to open the door the stacked stuff inside would have leapt out, possibly causing death by suffocation or crushing. The cobwebs had multiplied undisturbed for decades. There was no light in there: it was, in effect, an outside brick cupboard. Once this was clear we could put things in it such as wellies and paint and items which would not be damaged by damp; the type of stuff which was taking over the kitchen.

I asked Ant to start clearing the coalhouse. It was too dusty for me, and while he did that, I could sort the rest of the stuff. He removed six large squashed cardboard boxes, an old shirt and a few old pairs of tights and then stopped and wandered round the garden. I asked him what the problem was. He said he was worried he'd get shouted at for throwing out the cardboard, because Dad sometimes used it to light the fire.

I realised that the whole clearing up thing was really upsetting him. Dad has always been prone to nasty fits of temper and as Ant lived with him, he often suffered the sharp end of them. At least I could walk away. I asked a further three times for him to help me clear, before realising it was quicker to just do it myself. My poor brother was terrified he'd get into trouble for throwing stuff out. I, too, knew the clearing up thing would cause huge unpleasantness but somebody had to take the lead and see the situation for what it was. It was a nasty job but somebody had to do it. That somebody was me.

I put on a dust mask, grabbed everything remaining and chucked it on the grass. Something small and furry with a long tail scampered out of one of the boxes. No time to panic though. I yanked at the pile of stuff, getting covered in coal dust and large spiders. I don't mind spiders, which was just as well because some of those in that coal house were monsters. It was the dust I had to get away from. I found some of my teenage clothes and even my old school bag. There were more of my Mum's tights, a welly boot which was so disintegrated I was able to rip it open with my hands, some string, more bags, cardboard, spiders, spiders and more spiders. I kept pulling and found a nest and a second little furry fella scarpered sharpish. Most of what we found was stuff which the rest of the family had thrown out years before.

I wondered if Dad had *ever* thrown *anything* out. I remembered visiting him about five years ago. He'd been upset because, apparently, he'd been told off. He'd gone to the local shops and had put a carrier bag full of garden clay into the small bin mounted on the lampost outside the Post Office. A shopkeeper came out and told him not to do that because they had campaigned long and hard for the bin to keep the area clean from litter. The angry shopkeeper said they were not happy with him filling it with garden rubble. I suspected it wasn't the first time. His argument was that the bin was for public use and he was a member of the public. He was extremely upset by the shopkeeper's attitude. What right did they have to tell him where he could or could not put his rubbish?

I made a mental note to wear a hat and dark glasses if I ever had to go out in public with him. The question "Why did he have a bag of garden clay at the shop?" remains unanswered, although it appears he believed that the council would not take it if he put it in his bin.

At 2pm Ant reminded me of the time. As usual, I'd forgotten to eat anything all day. I had an hour and a half to go home, wash, eat, nip to the shop for something for tea, print off the DVLA form, take it to Dad in the hospital and get to work.

I was at the hospital only half an hour later. Dad was asleep. I poked him gently. He was upset at being woken.

'Do you want me to sit up?' he asked crossly.

'Well, I can talk to you better if you do.' I waited for him to sit up. He started to drift off again.

'Dad ~ I've got the form for you to sign. I went to the shop, got some printer ink and printed it off from my computer for you.'

'Oh right,' he said, 'I'd better sign it for you then.' He made an exaggeratedly gigantic effort to sit up. 'Right, where do you want me to sign?' He said this as if *he* were doing *me* a favour ~ and, naturally, not a word of thanks.

I told him I'd have to leave really soon, that I had just come in to bring him his church newsletter and the DVLA form to sign for the car tax refund.

'But you've only just got here.'

'Yes Dad, I know. I've been at the house since eight this morning and I didn't realise what the time was. I have to be in work by three and I'm working until nine thirty tonight.'

'Yes,' he said. 'It's amazing how time flies when you're enjoying yourself.'

I wasn't sure if this was his attempt at sarcasm or humour but it didn't go down too well. I stood to leave.

'When will I see you next?' he asked.

'Tuesday evening.'

'Yes, Tuesday. What time?'

'Tuesday evening.'

Blank stare.

'Tuesday evening, Dad! Tuesday. Evening.'

'Tuesday. Yes. What time?'

'IN THE EVENING. TUESDAY EVENING. I'll be out all day so I'll come in the EVENING!'

'What about the evening?'

I left. He hobbled to the ward door to watch me walk down the corridor.

I didn't look back.

# Chapter 7

It was fortunate this whole scenario happened in the summer because I could leave stuff on the lawn overnight. Thankfully the days that summer were long and dry giving me lots of daylight hours in which to work. Was this luck or some other force? I wonder. Living in Wales and having this much dry weather was bordering on the miraculous.

The garden was large and dust free, often sunny and with fresh air that was sadly lacking in the house. I could see later that I was making every excuse possible to stay in the garden and not have to go inside the house. The garden became my office. I had organised piles everywhere; stuff to go for recycling, stuff to go in the bin, stuff yet to be sorted, stuff to go back inside, valuable stuff and unidentifiable stuff. There was a "that just may be important" pile, a "that used to be mine pile" and finally a "very important; to be taken home with me to look at" pile.

Items in that last pile included long lost family photographs, letters I'd written home when I was travelling abroad, my grandparents' passports, a share certificate in my name and some of my personal stuff which had resurfaced in the clear out after being lost for over twenty years.

One of the most interesting items I found that day was an old hard backed, lined notebook. When I first checked I thought it was one of the books my mum had made notes in when she was studying for her Open University degree. I was about to throw it onto the paper recycling pile, until, flicking through it, I realised it was her personal diary, begun about nine months before I was born. The first entry was about how she broke the news to her younger sister and her mother that she was expecting me. It was obvious she was over the moon to be having her first baby. I know she had waited such a long time for that moment. This was one book to be kept carefully and treasured. It was an exciting discovery. I'd hoped to bring back some of my childhood memories and gain more of an insight into the kind of person my mother really was, together with her thoughts and feelings at the time. I was thrilled and so excited at the find.

Ploughing on with the coal house I found more of Mum's tights. They seemed to have weathered well over the past 25 years and still hadn't disintegrated. I must say though that when she wore them, I don't remember them being yellow and orange. I was sure they were typical "American Tan".

Some hours later, after dealing with plenty more huge spiders, lots of dust and more nesting fragments, the coal house was empty and Oggy, my little Toyota Rav4 car, was completely full.

The recycling centre and skip were about a mile away and with the windows open I could just about handle being wedged into the driver's seat. If I held my breath the musty smell was almost bearable. I also had two car batteries in the boot which I'd found in the garden, together with twenty or so of the prehistoric food tins from a few days before, any of which could explode at any second in the back of my poor little car.

I turned the ignition key and "Click", followed by silence. Oggy refused to start. No surprise really. If I'd been a car and had all that junk on board, I too would have refused to start. I had a silent word with her, I suggested the sooner she started the sooner the stuff would be gone. I sat and prayed to the god of Toyotas for her to start. That, along with the single blessing that Dad's house was at the top of a hill, meant I finally got her jump-started.

The funny little man at the tip nodded at me.

'Back again?' he asked.

'Yes,' I said 'and there'll be a few more visits too.' Boy, was *that* the understatement of the year!

~

I needed a break from the mountain so the family managed to get away for a few days. The holiday was booked months before and I'd promised the kids that despite everything, I'd go. I had been feeling so guilty about not being able to spend time with them since their granddad's accident. The break was meant to be for seven days but I came home after only four. I had to get back for the house. I was worried in case some doctor decided they wanted Dad out of hospital.

The day after I got home I had a full day at the mountain. I hadn't slept much for several nights because of everything running through my head. I had taken Mum's diary away with me. There were a few pre-me moments noted in there, such as 'I hope I can get the baby's room totally clear for when she/he is born'. It's not totally clear what it was full of but I assume it was Dad's junk. Also, "He has been amusing himself with his stamp collection today after mowing the lawn". Both comments were rather poignant with hindsight.

It was always hard to work out a plan of attack once I got to the house. Perhaps *Hoarder's Block* was a real issue. Although I'd already made a small start, an outsider looking at it would never know I'd even been in there let alone spent so many hours clearing it. The kitchen was by now down to about a fifth of the volume of clutter it had been but there was still too much mess by far.

I wondered whether it was best to wait for the health assessor to come round first but common sense told me the pro-active approach was the most logical plan of attack. I decided to clear one room completely so there would be somewhere to put excess stuff. I had a choice of two rooms, neither of which had been used in many years and therefore neither would have had anything inside that Dad was likely to need.

The first room had been my bedroom when I was a kid. The other was the "playroom". Playroom! Ha ha! It was supposed to be for Ant and me to play in when we were kids, though I don't remember ever being able to do that because it was always full of stuff. I remember there was a copper pipe through the wall between the playroom and the kitchen. We used to roll marbles through it from one room to another which provided *hours* of fun back in the late 1960's. There were no computers back then!

The playroom had a wood block floor and was located right at the front of the house on the ground floor. The mess was at least halfway up the level of the window and looked terrible from the road. Somewhere in there was my mother's sewing machine which I'd been asking Dad to find for me for twenty years or more. I figured this room would the best one to clear first and then it could be used to put "keep" stuff in.

The other room, my childhood bedroom, was on the top floor next to the bathroom. This could be used as a temporary bedroom for Dad when he came out of hospital, providing he was able to climb the stairs. His bedroom wasn't suitable: the bed was covered in junk and papers. The floor was hidden under a six inch layer of newspapers that had fallen from surrounding piles over the past twenty years and not been picked up. These made the floor slippery and unstable to walk on and if he needed a paramedic, doctor or nurse in the night, the paper-covered floor would not have been safe.

My old bedroom was like a scene from *"The Lion, The Witch and The Wardrobe".* The whole of the door frame had been used for the previous ten or so years as a wardrobe rail. There were numerous jackets hanging there. If the coats were pulled apart you could just see the room the other side. This was very much what I imagined Narnia to be like although there would have been more snow and less clutter. There could almost have been a whole lost world in there.

I decided to ask Dad which room he thought would be best to clear for him to sleep in. He still appeared to be under the impression the hospital staff would let him out to clear the house himself. He, apparently, was living on a different planet from the rest of us. He hadn't cleared anything for the previous twenty years and had only added to the mess. Why he thought anyone would believe he'd ever change was unclear.

He told me many times I was not to touch *anything* in the living room as it was all apparently sorted into piles ready for him to do his tax return. Interestingly, his tax return had been his priority item on his *to do* list for the past twenty years. It was also a priority over my mother's probate nineteen years ago. That took him ten years to do. Of course a tax return needs to be done every year but he had an accountant to do his ~ so all he had to do was provide the figures.

I broached the subject of where to start a clear-out: 'Dad, I think, for now, I should sort out just one room in the house for you to use as a bedroom. It would surely be sensible to do this now rather than wait for you to be told the house has to be totally cleared before you can come home.' I wanted to reassure him that I wouldn't touch his stuff in the living room. I said, 'I'm *not* talking about the living room. I won't touch *any* of your stuff in the living room. I *know* all your paperwork is organised in the living room so I won't touch that.'

He looked at me as if I were a bit stupid and said, 'I don't want you to go tidying stuff up because...'

I interrupted him. 'Dad! I will *not* touch the living room. I *know* your stuff is in there. However, I think I should at least start clearing the playroom or my old bedroom for you to come home.'

I saw him hackling up for an argument. I knew exactly what he was about to say, so I said, as loudly and as clearly as I possibly could, 'I will *not* touch the living room – only the two unused rooms.'

He started to say 'I don't want you to touch the living room.' He clearly hadn't heard (or, perhaps, listened to) a single word I'd said. He was too pre-occupied with his own speech which, as ever, was of far more importance than anything I could ever possibly have to say. Although I spoke slowly and clearly and a BBC news reader at half speed couldn't have been any clearer, I was still convinced he hadn't listened to a thing I'd said.

I frequently get the impression he doesn't listen to me because he doesn't believe I have anything intelligent or important to say. He often acts as if I'm ten years old. I said, 'Dad! Just the playroom or my old room ~ which one would be the best?'

He shouted loudly over me 'I wish you would listen to me girl!' He looked at me as if I had just crawled out of the gutter and continued, 'I don't want you to touch any of my paperwork in the living room because...'

At this point I wondered if I would be justified in giving him a smack in the chops. However, reason overcame me and I decided it was easier to let him carry on with his speech, which I had heard *so* many times before that I can repeat it verbatim.

I sighed, clenched my teeth and stared hard at the pattern on his hospital blanket. Letting him get on with it was the only way we could move on with the conversation. Until he'd said his bit, clearly he would not entertain anything I had to say.

He continued slowly, as if he was talking to some form of imbecile. 'It's all organised in there and I have all my paperwork laid out.'

I wanted to scream. I felt my blood pressure rising. I had to pinch myself to keep my latent axe murderess under control.

Dad was still clearly under the impression he'd be allowed out to clear the house himself. I  tried to point out that I wasn't even going to attempt to sort his paperwork out but that a thousand decomposing carrier bags, 60 margarine tubs, 137 Lidl weekly newsletters from 2006, Metro newspapers, old underpants, jar lids, countless broken odd shoes, thousands of corks, empty bottles, scrunched up old tissues, food tins up to fifteen years out of date, pots and pans where the non-stick was flaking so badly it was a health hazard, bits of string etc., can, by most people's definition of rubbish, be binned.

He said he'd obviously kept them all for some reason and suggested that perhaps the phone had rung while he was in the middle of reading each one.

It would have made it *so* much easier if I'd known I was doing this with his blessing and agreement. We both knew I'd have to do it someday so why wouldn't he let me help him now? He suggested I cleared the stairway and around his bed so that if a doctor needed to come in the night he could have entered the house safely.

I had taken photos of the mountain to show to the nurses on the ward. 'Dear me,' (or words to that effect), said the nurse. 'It's just like them shows on the telly! Does anyone really live like that for real?'  She then rushed off to empty a bedpan somewhere. The other nurse said her mother was a bit of a hoarder too. She said it wasn't possible to put her car in the garage any longer because there was so much stuff in there. *Clearly different ends of the hoarding spectrum,* I thought!

# Chapter 8

My cousin Jane met me at the mountain at 9am. She'd brought extra help in the form of her two boys Adam and Matthew. We decided that starting on the stairs would be the best plan because clearing these would make it possible to move stuff through the house.

I started sorting in the garden and Jane and the boys brought the stuff out to me in bags and boxes. Within minutes, Adam appeared with a box filled with a whole heap of stuff ~ tissues, bits of wood, corks, bottle tops, lids, more bits of wood, screws, receipts, coins, yet more bits of wood, old papers, and junk mail. In one box he had found a twenty pound note which he handed to me. And then another one, and then a ten pound note, two more twenties and two fives. I put all the notes safely in my bag. My intention was to add all the money up and give it to Dad in one go after he came out of hospital. I hoped this would have made him more careful and possibly tidier in future.

After two solid hours hard shifting and a trip to the skip, the garden was full and the stairs were empty. We moved a large bookcase from the top of the stairs together with all the books in it. The bookcase went to a friend of mine, 'Skip', who desperately needed a bookcase. I took all the books home to my own house to be sorted. I came across an old book by the ballroom dancer Victor Silvester. When I flicked through it I noticed it was autographed by the man himself and his entire band. I decided it should go in the *keep* pile along with a 1950s book of stamp collecting with a few sheets of about twenty mint 2d and 3d stamps inside.

At the bottom of a pile there was a batch of newspapers entitled "*Carpenters' and Builders' Weekly*" dated 1891. They were instructions for planning and building Victorian houses 120 years ago. I found them especially interesting because I was studying a three year carpentry course at college. I wondered whether my interest may have come from one of my ancestors. I have since found out that my paternal great grandmother was a carpenter/wood carver and my maternal great grandfather was a cabinet maker. I was thrilled to have discovered this information. I'd never have known if I hadn't found these papers. Yet another example of why I had to do this myself. I doubt anyone else would have bothered even to look twice at them.

That day we also found seventeen shoes, two of which were even a pair, bits of wood, bottles of wine, plastic bags, paper clips, television valves, five fluorescent bulbs, some silver, but now black, spoons, a lighthouse lamp, some tea towels, bits of wood, string, three dusty and solidified hand cream jars, twenty-three bars of soap, a few dusters, more bits of wood, plastic jugs, a ceramic tortoise, one plastic goat, an unopened book, pegs, a playing card, a woolly hat, three deceased spiders, eight margarine tubs, six cotton reels, three sets of Christmas lights, another colony of silverfish and some old pyjama bottoms.

Jane had a big car and offered to take stuff to my mate *Skip*'s house. *Skip* had become very needy over those few weeks.

The remainder of the prehistoric food tins and jars also went to their final destination. In one day we had got rid of about twelve large bags of rubbish and recycling just from the stairs and landing. It was finally possible to walk up the stairs *and* turn around at the top.

When I was young I could climb the stairs in the dark, despite there being room for only one foot on each stair. I knew where the spaces on each stair were - in between the piles of tinned pies, shoes, tins of paint and the rolled-up *new* carpet he'd put on the stairs on the day he bought it in 1974. He put it there to keep it from being damaged until the main bedroom was ready for it. It was still there forty years later, when he fell out of the tree.

The carpet was an in house joke with my friends back when I was a kid as it was there the whole time I was in school. I wondered what my school mates, some of them now grandparents, would have thought if they knew it was still there forty years later.

The stairs were now virtually clear. The only thing left was the carpet, now threadbare around the edges and very dusty. There was nowhere else for it to go so it stayed there until we found another place for it.

I left Ant with a big mess on the back garden lawn and took another heap of stuff to the skip on my way home. The little chappie there winked at me. At least, I think he winked at me ~ he had a squint so it could have been my imagination.

Later that day, after a full day at the mountain, I went to visit Dad in hospital. From his hospital bed, Dad proudly handed me three Metro free newspapers dated March 2013 and proudly announced, 'You can recycle these, I've finished with them.' This was a week after I'd taken him a bag of old papers for him to read through so he could feel as if he were doing his bit. He'd finished just three of them while he was lying in his hospital bed.

Calculating three a week times 876,264 papers would mean he would be about 1084 years old by the time he had read them all ~ and that was providing he acquired no more in the meantime.

Dad was clearly under the impression I had been *tidying* the house. I had no doubt that he being in hospital was the reason my progress was so good. I shuddered when I imagined him being at home while I was throwing stuff out. He'd be taking everything back out of the bin "to deal with later".

I was fairly confident he wouldn't be released before the end of the week: even so, all the recycling bags and items to go out had already been taken to the skip so that if he did come out of hospital unexpectedly, he wouldn't come home and throw a wobbly.

I mentioned to him that a friend had been helping me. He wasn't pleased about that as he didn't even trust me in his house, let alone one of my friends. He assumed anyone else would simply throw all his stuff out. As it happened it was me who was throwing things out but only if I was *sure* it was rubbish and also that I could live with the guilt trips I knew he would lavish on me. I wouldn't let anyone else throw anything out.

# Chapter 9

My friend Jackie came from Swindon to help me over the weekend. As soon as she learned about my situation she made plans to come and help. Jackie and I grew up in the same street together so she knew Dad really well and he knew her. She'd been in the house many times when we were kids, although she hadn't seen it for the previous twenty years or so.

Jackie brought everything down from my old bedroom. She must have gone up and down those stairs over a hundred times. There were more bits of wood, fluorescent tubes, bulbs, shoes, boxes, old papers, *three* mattresses and a divan bed base, twelve jumpers, a jacket, twenty identical new pairs of men's underpants, more shoes and the usual tat. We also found lots of spare bits for old televisions ~ brand new bits, still in their original boxes, for those televisions which nobody had anymore. Dad was the only person I knew who still had one.

We found lots and lots more of Dad's shoes. There were probably about fifty or sixty pairs or more spread all over the house and lots more single shoes which had been separated from their partners. We found all sorts of shoes, from summer sandals to winter shoes, cheap and nasty Spanish supermarket sandals to very posh looking designer leather numbers still in their original boxes. Some were well worn but most were new. All were black, brown or beige and of similar styles. I had no idea why anyone would want or need to buy so many shoes. We were amazed; after all he only had one pair of feet. I thought it was meant to be us girls who collected shoes. We joked Dad would give Imelda Marcos a run for her money.

Imelda! Now that was a very fitting nickname for him! We sat on the grass and laughed and laughed. It was a rare moment of laughter during those few weeks I can tell you!

Yes '*Imelda*' – it was perfect!

Bearing in mind it was my old bedroom we were clearing it was no surprise that we found bags and bags of Culture Club memorabilia. I had flags, tickets, books, programmes, badges, scrap books, newspaper cuttings, dolls and T-shirts. Did I throw them out? *Did I heck*! I didn't bring them home though, I left them there. A little bit of my history which meant so much at the time and which I still couldn't bear to bin. Did that mean I had hoarding tendencies? I sincerely hoped not.

I also found some black bed sheets. I think this was because the theme of my room was black and white everything with one colour at a time, usually to match my mood of the moment. The black and white spotted curtains were still hanging up in the window and the white and black spotted gift wrap sheets were still all over the walls. There were also two odd shoes, mine this time, which went straight in the bin along with my old leather cowboy boots. Interestingly the boots were almost identical to my favourite current pair in my cupboard at home.

In a box right at the back of my room I found a *huge* pile of poly pockets, full of more mint stamps in shillings and old pence. There were sheets and sheets of them. I put these in a very safe place as I suspected they may have been valuable. In the bottom of the box was a small brass camping stove.

Every box brought out had memories in it. We found the old Christmas box and spent a while reminiscing about our childhood Christmases. The big moment in our house was always when Dad got the *Bristol Cream Sherry* cardboard box from the attic and all the familiar decorations came out. It was always traditional in our house that on Christmas *Eve,* and never before, after clearing a three foot square space, Dad would go and dig up the tree from the garden and put it in a bucket of damp soil. We'd then wrap silver foil around the base and decorate the tree.

On either Christmas or Boxing Day, a few neighbours would come over for a mince pie and a sherry, the tree lights would be turned on as the radio played traditional carols live from the cathedral. We'd be allowed to eat *Quality Street* chocolates from the tin all day.

As each year went by there was less and less room for a tree in the living room until there was barely room left for a pine needle. The festive lights simply stayed up all year and were switched on at Christmas. Deflated and sad looking flaps of latex with dusty ribbons hung from the lights all year round, once proud and jolly balloons, they became ignored and abandoned. Nobody even cared enough to take them down. The decorations box had not been seen for many years after it was put away one year.

Christmas paper from way back was buried randomly in different rooms. Dad used to peel off paper very carefully from gifts he'd been given, fold it and put it aside. The paper would then become dusty, dog eared and tired. Months or even years later his family would find the same sheet of paper roughly wrapped around their gifts from him, crudely stuck together with electrical masking tape. Usually he wasn't able to find the paper so an old carrier bag also stuck with masking tape was his gift wrap of choice. One year he gave his granddaughters some chocolates for their birthday in August wrapped in Christmas paper. Often he bought pretty dresses for his granddaughters while he was on holiday. These were lost by the time Christmas came around. By the time their birthdays came the clothes were too small.

As the hoarding got worse year by year the Christmas tree was brought in later and later because it always took a while to clear a space for it. One year it didn't come in until Christmas Day itself, just after lunch.

A few years later it was Boxing Day before he got round to digging it up. After that we never had a tree in the house. There was no longer any room.

The same tree was still in the garden that day we were sorting. It was now about fifteen feet high.

Gradually as the house got more buried under his hoarded stuff the neighbours were reduced to a select close few friends and family who came round at Christmas. Eventually nobody came round at all.

# Chapter 10

After a whole day of clearing we had definitely broken the back of the mess in my old bedroom. The skip pile in the garden was huge. The "*keep me*" pile was worryingly bigger than I could really justify but I needed to keep some things back to maintain the illusion that I was not throwing *all* his stuff out. We made a total of five trips to the skip in two cars. This was all from just one bedroom.

I was still worried that the hospital would release Imelda without warning me. I was afraid he'd arrive home one day to find a huge pile of recycling bags in the garden which, of course, he'd *have* to check through. For this reason they all went to the skip the same day instead of waiting for the weekly collection.

We went back to my house at about 7pm, grabbing a pizza on the way home, showered and headed off to the hospital for the daily visit. Jackie had known Imelda since she was four. Although she was only six months older than me, in his eyes she had achieved adult status, whereas I got the feeling even though I was the wrong side of forty, with my own children, he still saw me as a small insignificant child. Jackie did some straight talking with him. She told him how it was. She said we had to be ruthless if he was *ever* to be allowed to come home.

I remembered that it had taken over *ten years* to sort out Mum's probate after she died, even though I nagged him about it weekly. His excuse was that he was getting around to it, or that he couldn't find the paperwork, or even that his tax return was more urgent. Year after year went by. People told me I needed to get him to do it, as if I didn't know and wasn't already doing what I could. I couldn't force him to do it. Despite all his urgent paperwork he still found time to ensure the garden was immaculate and vegetables planted, tended and harvested. The garden took priority over the probate, the tax return and the mess inside the house.

Eventually, after ten years, I took matters into my own hands. I booked an appointment at the probate office and rang him to tell him I was picking him up for the appointment. When it was done, after only an hour, he said, 'I didn't think it would be that simple.' I could have shot him on the spot.

While Jackie had words with Imelda in the hospital, I spoke to a nurse at the ward reception desk. I'd taken lots more photos on my mobile phone of the house and showing her these appeared to work. Perhaps she had personal experience of a hoarder. The other nurses all gathered to look and express their horror. They said they hadn't thought for a minute that his house would be like that ~ he appeared *so normal*.

The nurse told me that a residential health assessor would have to go and inspect his house and this would probably be done the following week. Imelda had already been assessed but the house had to be fully assessed as well. Finally, somebody seemed to be taking the issue seriously.

The following day Jackie and I were up, dressed, breakfasted and over at the mountain early. We got stuck straight in. Within an hour we had the three single mattresses outside on the drive, together with the divan bed base from my old bedroom. One mattress was originally from the guest bedroom in my grandfather's flat. He died in 1979, but it was the newest of the three. The other two appeared to be stuffed with horsehair. I recognised one of them as the one I slept on for at least the first fifteen years of my life. Considering my extreme allergy to animal fur and to horses in particular, I wondered if anyone ever put two and two together and realised the impact it was having on my health.

By midday poor Jackie had been up and down the stairs more times that weekend than I had been in the previous twenty years. The room was now 90% empty. The feeling was amazing. We opened the window wide for the first time in over twenty years and let the fresh air pour in. The bedroom carpet was unearthed and vacuumed by a large vacuum cleaner which had clearly not been used in years. Imelda had a handheld vacuum which was used daily to get rid of the moths but the big one was not used, primarily because it had been buried but also because there was not enough visible floor to clean nor space to wheel it around.

We drove home to my house listening to the Pet Shop Boys, "*It's a sin*". "*In the bin,*" we sang. The mood was good!

# Chapter 11

I dropped the kids off at school on the first day back after the holidays and headed straight to base camp at the mountain. Ant was at work so it was just me and the dog.

I'd planned to start on the play-room, but the hallway was still too cluttered to get through safely, especially carrying big items. I didn't want any of my friends getting injured, so I had to clear the hallway first. Everything was so precariously balanced that it was like the wooden block game *Jenga*; if the wrong thing was moved the whole lot was likely to come down.

From the hallway I picked up three jars of unlabelled substances ~ possibly paint in a previous life. The jars' contents had separated and the jars were covered in a thick layer of sticky dust. Imelda would have walked past them in the hallway on a daily basis for the past thirty years or so. They weren't buried at the back of a pile, but on full view right at the front.

The dust was flying everywhere and I was glad I had my dust suit and mask on. I picked up a box, carried it outside, sorted it and went back in for another, over and over.

The paperwork needed to be sorted as it came out. If it was from the top of a pile, i.e. recent, I couldn't bin it as Imelda would have known it was there. Bits at the back or at the bottom were likely to be over fifteen years old and I was able to be a bit more flippant with these.

There seemed to be so many boxes full of bits of wire, spanners, screwdrivers, sockets, screws, nails and bits of *stuff* with wires coming out. The paperwork could have been anything ~ all mixed in the same pile. In just one pile there were letters from 2008 together with Lidl magazines from 2005, some unopened *"Which"* magazines, two bank statements from 2010 and two shareholder reports from 2012. Next to this pile there were shareholder reports from companies which hit the deck years ago, on top of envelopes full of labels from soup and spaghetti tins.

When I dug around a bit deeper I found five "Order of Service" leaflets dating back years from funerals of different people who had ascended the ladder of life for the final time and not come down it again as quickly as Imelda did a few weeks ago.

The health assessor was due at 3pm. I'd been reassured that she'd have visited the house anyway even if I hadn't taken the photos to show the hospital staff. She needed to check the height of the toilet, stair rails, and bed. I was glad they told me this as I'd started to feel guilty for mentioning the mess to the nurses at all.

The phone rang while I was at base camp; it was Imelda.

'Oh!' he said, 'Good, I hoped I'd catch you. Are we expecting a visitor this afternoon?' I confirmed that the assessor was due at three. Imelda then started rambling on about the downstairs toilet as the flush didn't work. 'Simple to fix!' he told me. He suggested my husband may have been able to fix it. Oh, how this wound me up! *I* was the one who did the plumbing in our house!

After taking a course in plumbing I'd successfully fitted a new basin in my own bathroom, taken out a toilet in a flat, removed a sink and a bath, fitted isolation valves and fixed my taps. I'd told him that ~ many times. Why not? I was proud of myself! This just proved my point that he didn't ever listen to a word I said. He believed, for whatever reason, that it should be the male who did the fixing and he obviously took little, if any, interest in anything I ever told him.

Then he mentioned the carpet on the stairs. He said it was dangerous. He was referring to the one *fitted* to the stairs and not the rolled up one. As the stairs had been loaded with junk either side for so long, the carpet had been subject to extra wear and tear and had become extremely threadbare in the middle, right through to the wood in some places. He said ~ get this ~ he knew I could fit carpets and so thought that between us we could get it sorted.

I reminded him I had to wear a mask to even go into the house and there was no way I could handle his dusty, prehistoric carpet! He chose to suffer selective deafness at this point. I screamed down the phone that I was unable to go into his house without a mask.

He said, 'You're unable to go in without a man?' Whether he was attempting to be amusing or if he was just doing it to annoy me wasn't clear.

*Twelve* times I had to say, '*MASK* Dad ~ I can't go in without a *mask!*' I finally screamed it down the phone with such frustration I almost choked on my own fury.

Finally he got what I was saying and he replied. 'That's OK ~ we can get you a mask.' As if *he* was doing *me* a favour. I began to appreciate why some people turned to alcohol for comfort.

At this point I honestly didn't think Imelda and I were living on the same planet. He was worried he wouldn't be allowed home because of the toilet and the stair carpet. Clearly that was akin to worrying that your eyeliner may run in a tsunami.

I'd just filled my car with the latest cargo of junk when the health assessor arrived. I'd spoken to her the day before and had warned her of what she was likely to find. She said she'd seen it all before. I told her I doubted it. She said she was primarily coming to check the height of the toilet and the bed and assess whether a stair rail was needed.

To say the assessor was horrified doesn't do justice to the range of expressions that flitted over her face. Speechless, dumbstruck, shocked, flabbergasted and overwhelmed may have been more accurate. I couldn't tell if she was amused or horrified. She said 'Ah!' a lot and, 'My goodness!' and 'You really have a huge job here.'

Yes, I know. Thanks!

She said she would have assessed the stairs ~ if she could have seen them. Likewise she would have assessed the bed ~ had she been able to get within ten feet of it safely. She reckoned the mess had become so much a part of the house and his life within it that he simply didn't even see it any more. I had to agree.

Just as she left, my friend Andrea from work arrived to help, armed with more Ikea bags, and got stuck straight in. She filled the bags and brought the stuff out which I sorted into three piles - recycle, keep and bin. The bin pile started looking rather healthy as did the recycle pile. Sadly the keep pile was also bigger than I would have liked but all this stuff belonged to Imelda not me. To be cautious, bearing in mind this stuff wasn't mine, a further pile emerged. Anything on this *not sure* pile was kept. I had to decide which items were important from somebody else's lifetime of hoarding. Imelda had no real say in the matter. The minute I asked him about something specific and brought it to his attention I knew I'd never be able to throw it out.

By 6:30 we'd had enough. I finished loading Oggy and went home via the recycling centre. My poor little car was stuffed full. There was barely enough room for yet another old spark plug. The little skip man must have been on tea break. A bit of a relief really ~ I thought he may have tried to start charging me soon.

I came home, had a quick bite and then took two of the kids to the hospital to visit their granddad. Imelda immediately asked what the assessor had said. I told him he wouldn't be allowed home until the house was clear. He was under the impression that he'd be able to come home in the daytime but would have to return to the hospital at night. I explained that was *never* going to happen. He started having a go at me then as if it was *my* fault he wasn't allowed home.

Ignoring that, I gave him his bank balance slip. I'd been to his house to get his bank card and then driven to two cash machines on the way to the hospital as the first was out of order.

I said, 'Here's your slip, Dad. I couldn't get a statement as the bank was closed.'

He took it from me. 'What's this?'

'It's your bank balance slip, Dad ~ the one you asked me for ~ one bank machine wasn't working so I had to go to another.'

'Is this a receipt?''

'No ~ it's your *bank balance.*'

'Well, that's no good is it? It doesn't have the transactions on.'

# Chapter 12

After the school run I had a quick cup of coffee and headed over to the mountain. The plan was to finish clearing the playroom. Most of the contents of the room had been there for probably the best part of twenty years. Jane came round at ten and she brought the stuff out. The dust was horrendous and I couldn't go inside the house. We opened both front and back doors and left them open all day to clear the air. The garden was in a shocking state. It was a strange thing but in the garden, a space about fifty metres by twenty metres was full of stuff which had come from a room about four or five metres square.

I found many old Christmas cards which had been sent to Dad, together with the sympathy cards received after Mum passed away. Oddly, and perhaps somewhat revealingly, I found a birthday card to Dad signed "Glenda's parents". Hmmm. Surely the norm would be to sign "Mum and Dad" or possibly "Fred and Phyllis".

There was a box marked *cardboard*. Inside was a load of flattened cereal boxes with covers from annual shareholder reports. Why had he kept them? There were empty cereal boxes stuffed in one box neatly together with A4 envelopes ~ all used and empty. Other random boxes contained stuff like lots of screwed up tissues, margarine lids, some old fuses, an old light bulb, a cut up shoe and a huge jar of broad bean seeds.

In one of the boxes amongst all the junk were my grandfather's solicitor's letters from the purchase of his house ~ all together in the same box with old shoe linings and bits of string. There were also letters with a diary written by my grandfather in 1913 when he was travelling around South Africa. These were in with bits of old wire, more shoes, more green garden clogs, lots of photos, old maps, old magazines and a bottle of whisky dated 1949. Next to these was a box of expensive wine.

Loose on top of these boxes we found a pair of men's scraggy underpants. Hopefully these had been washed and used as dusters.

There were pots and pots of old paint. A broken chainsaw in three pieces evidently beyond logical repair lay in a box. There were smaller boxes containing hundreds of screws and nails, my old school books, my mother's wool coat, another old record player, a box of 78rpm vinyl records, a large wooden elephant complete with a gong and a hitting stick, some razor blades, lots of live silverfish, some airline biscuits dated 2002 and airline earphones, many bits of old televisions with wires sticking out and two small bottles of mercury!

I was a little worried about the bottles of mercury. What the heck did he have those for? They were very old ceramic bottles with a cork lid and had evidently been there for a very long time. The two bottles were about the size of a salt cellar used at the average family table. I left them there as I didn't know what to do with them. I thought they may have been something to do with televisions. Underneath everything we found a small empty chest of drawers.

After Jane had gone, one of the neighbours came over as I was sitting down sorting through a pile of papers. I knew her well as she had lived there many years. We had a nice long chat and she spoke about my Mum who she told me she fondly remembered.

So many people told me they had such good memories of my mother ~ apparently she was lovely, patient, gentle and kind. Yet again I heard the story about Mum sneaking stuff into the neighbours' dustbins because, if she threw anything out, Dad would rifle through and extract whatever she'd thrown out and take it back inside. This neighbour said my Mum had been struggling with this issue since before I was born. The neighbour then brought me a hot cup of coffee, some ginger cake and a biscuit for which I was extremely grateful. When she brought them over it was 4pm and I hadn't eaten anything, other than some crisps my cousin brought me, since breakfast ~ and breakfast had only been a coffee.

By 5pm there was stuff all over the lawn. I wanted to ensure the now empty room was cleaned and dust free before the stuff went back inside. Ant did this after I left. The big question was what to do with all the stuff outside? It was counter-productive to put it all back in only to carry it out again the next morning. The important items were taken inside ~ old photographs, letters and all the items which might have been damaged if they got damp overnight. The rest had to stay outside until the following day. I'd wanted to take the next day off from the mountain, but had to cancel that idea as I couldn't leave the stuff outside for a whole day in case it rained.

At last the playroom was empty apart from a chest full of tools and two tool boxes. Lots of stuff would be going back in the room the following day but 70% of it had gone. This room was the one chosen as a storage room for the junk in the rest of the house.

The next day I'd planned to put the sorted stuff back in the house which would leave us free to start on one of the bigger rooms later in the week. I hoped the weather held.

# Chapter 13

My day off never materialised because I'd been offered help the following day. I needed to accept every offer I had because I never knew when the help might run out ~ or, indeed, when Imelda would be released. He'd been nagging the hospital every day to release him. The hospital was also eager not to keep patients in longer than was strictly necessary.

I had to organise the house with the things I thought Imelda might need at the top and the front. It wasn't good utilisation of labour to ask my friends to put the stuff back in as they had no idea where things went.

I had to maximise the help I had. The only thing I couldn't do because of my dust allergy was take the existing stuff out of the house. As soon as the dust started flying I had to go outside and the last thing anybody needed was for me to have to go into hospital with a dust induced asthma attack.

On a few occasions I had more than one helper. On these days within a very short time, my helpers started bringing out far more bags than I could sort. Inevitably they'd notice there was more building up than I could cope with and they'd kindly offer to help with the sorting. This made it unbelievably stressful for me because I knew I couldn't let anyone else sort his stuff. I knew everyone was trying to be helpful and that they had my interest at heart. I certainly didn't want to appear ungrateful or upset anybody. However, if they did sort, I then felt obliged to take a mental note of which bags they had sorted – inevitably they would *sort* at least twice as fast as I could.

I knew the importance of checking everything; each sheet of paper, every single envelope, not just piles of envelopes. Their wonderful helpfulness meant, sadly, that I had to identify and isolate the bags they had sorted to put aside and sort again later after they'd gone. This made even more work for me but I was so scared of upsetting someone and making them feel I was ungrateful that I just dealt with it.

One day a friend of Ant's came round to offer help and he told me he had *sorted* piles of stuff. I put his *sorted* bags separate from mine. Later, when he'd gone, I went through these *sorted* bags and discovered an envelope which contained £10 and £20 notes, an envelope containing a new but out of date credit card and three bank statements. Nobody on the planet understands a hoarder better than their family. The buck stopped with me and I couldn't promise I would sort stuff personally if I let other people throw it out. I couldn't let him look for stuff which I couldn't *guarantee* hadn't been thrown out.

I eventually only asked my closest friends to help, friends who I knew would respect my wishes and let me do it *my way* and not push me. I specifically only asked for two hours help at a time to be able to deal with it all without becoming overwhelmed. I stayed long after my friends had gone to sort by myself taking my time to go through every single newspaper to check there were no inserts such as share certificates or £20 notes tucked between the pages. To others it wasn't logical to put or find important documents in such places and so they didn't look for them. I was used to nothing being logical and was more or less raised to expect the unexpected.

Imelda would have been horrified had he known that someone he didn't know personally was in his house. I wasn't there because I wanted to be or because I was asked to be. I was there as there was simply nobody else who could or would have done it properly. Anyone else would have gone in with a skip and a spade which on the face of it was the most tempting option but under the circumstances would have had devastating consequences on Imelda. I simply had no choice.

I was always mindful that none of the stuff belonged to me so I didn't have the right to throw it out. I wouldn't have been happy if someone came in to my house when I wasn't there and threw my stuff out.

On the other hand, however, Imelda was in hospital with a broken back and I was therefore doing what any daughter would be expected to do and helping him *tidy* his house so he was able to come home and be able to move about safely. However, this house couldn't be "tidied" because there was no space to put anything. Things had to go so other stuff could have a place. Everything was very precariously balanced on top of everything else.

He had bought things, lost them in the mess and then bought more because he had forgotten he had the originals. We had by then found about 127 shoes. Some had a partner, some were worn out so the sole was split, some were brand new leather, some were nasty plastic, and some were sad sandals. One shoe I dragged out from the bottom of a six foot pile split into two when I flexed it ~ it had been there so long it had solidified.

Apart from the layers of green shirts, there were new trousers and jumpers in original packaging or in their original carrier bags all over the place that he had bought and then forgotten about. I dug out a chip fryer, a toaster and a steamer that day ~ all new in their boxes. There was also a bag of loose change ~ it had ½p coins, pesetas, francs and *new* 5p pieces twice the size of current 5p pieces.

I had to decide whether each and every item should be kept or thrown. I found more new stamps in sheets, books from 1908 and maps of Cardiff from 1918. I found silver spoons and an egg cup set in solid silver in with a box of rusty old nails. Everything had to be so carefully checked.

There were a few things I was unsure whether I could throw out. I thought I'd test the water and ask Imelda about one or two of them. I wondered what would happen if I asked him about them ~ thereby giving him the final word and so allowing him to have some kind of control. I knew this could backfire as if he hadn't already been aware the items were there then just mentioning them would bring them to his attention and this in itself would render them impossible to throw out. I decided to test the water with just one or two items.

First was the old chainsaw, the plastic handle end was broken off, the chain part was broken and the motor was exposed. I'd found it in a large box in the front room right at the bottom of a pile. It had probably been there at least fifteen years. There was also another old record player in the same room which had been sitting on top of a pile of stuff right at the back. I decided to ask him if I could throw just these two items out.

At 2.30 I went to visit Imelda in the hospital. He was fast asleep on the bed. I gently poked him awake.

'Uh err uugghh,' he said. 'Are you on your own?'

'Yes, I'm on my way to work.'

'Didn't you bring Ant?'

'No, Dad. I'm on my way to work.'

'You could've picked him up and he could've walked home.'

'I didn't have time to pick him up Dad. I went home after working at your house, showered and I've now come to visit you.'

'Yes, but you didn't bring him.'

'No, I'm going to work.'

'Oh!' I thought I detected some disappointment.

Pointed *silence...*

'Any news?' he asked.

'About what? ~ I've been at the house all day, every day.'

'Yes, yes I know that, but is there any news from the health assessor?'

'Only what she told you ~ you can't come home until the house is clear.'

'Oh that is bloody ridiculous, what a load of old nonsense!'

'Dad, that's *them* saying that, not me.'

'Bloody ridiculous ~ don't they realise I can't sort the house out while I'm stuck in here?'

I *so* wanted to point out he was now retired and had been in the house every day for the past forty years and it had certainly never come anywhere even remotely close to the definition of *clear*. I bit my tongue.

I decided that might be a good moment to broach the subject of the chain saw and the record player.

'Dad ~ there's a broken chain saw in pieces in the playroom, is it OK if I throw it out?'

'No of course it bloody isn't, I use that in the garden!'

'No, Dad. Not the one you use ~ that's safe in the shed. This is one from the playroom, it has no chain, the handle is snapped off and the motor is exposed. It's been there a long time and is covered in dust. It's in several pieces.'

'Well you can't just throw it out ~ put it in the garage.'

'Dad, there's no room in the garage.'

'Well then put it in the shed.'

'There is no room in the shed.'

'Well put it in the bloody greenhouse then ~ I know it's a new concept to you!'

'Dad, why do you need it? It's old, broken and it's taking up space, you've got one in the shed which works so why can't this one go out?'

'Because I need to see it to make a bloody decision don't I? It may just need a new blade.'

'OK Dad. You win. What about the record player?'

'What bloody record player? There's one in the kitchen ~ unless you've thrown that out already. I bet you have thrown that out ~ haven't you?' (As it happens I had, but this was a different one).

'Dad, this one was in the playroom. You already have a record player in the lounge which is working *and* one in the kitchen. They don't even make records anymore.'

'Again I need to see it to be able to tell ~ oh *why* are you being so bloody difficult?'

'Dad, we need to get rid of some stuff so they'll let you come home...' I tailed off deciding that to attempt to continue the conversation would be totally and utterly futile. I wanted to hit him with a big stick. Luckily I couldn't find one.

He piped up, 'The social worker said I may be able to stay with you until I can go home, but I told her that it's two buses from your house to mine so that wouldn't be practical.' Now I wanted to hit the social worker with an even larger stick. There was no way on earth that he was ever going to stay in my house. Unless they wanted a murder on their hands.

I stood up (he was still lying down). 'I have to go now.' I said, 'I doubt I'll be in tomorrow as I'm working again and I'll be at the house until about two.'

'Yes,' he said. Did I hear *thank you*? No, I most definitely did not!

I walked out, past the nurses, wondering if they had any idea of what he was really like. He could be a real charmer when he wanted and all the ladies seemed to fall for it. Me, however, he treated as some inferior species, an irritating moron without the maturity, intelligence, common sense or ability to choose what to keep and what to bin. He didn't recognise me as a fully functioning adult who (at the time at least!) still had all her faculties/marbles, had a decent , tidy house, three kids under ten, a job and a life and was due to begin the second year of a carpentry course, full time, at college the following week.

I also had to handle the guilt of throwing things away: things that didn't belong to me but which needed to go out. I knew Ant was terrified that I'd throw something away that Imelda would miss and of having to endure the ensuing mood/temper that would inevitably follow for weeks ~ if not months. I didn't like that mountain. I didn't ask to climb that mountain, I didn't like being at that mountain. I had no choice but to spend every waking hour at the sodding mountain to the detriment of my family, other people and important activities in my life at that time. It had not been a good day. I went to work at 3:30 with a monster knot in my stomach which refused to untie.

# Chapter 14

I was at the mountain early. The health assessor was due to phone at 1:30 and I wanted to be able to tell her there had been a vast improvement. I wasn't sure what her expectations were but at least she was fully aware of the scale of the job in hand.

My friends Rhian and Cath came round to help prepare for the assessor. As much as I explained about the situation and put details and photos online, this was both cathartic and helped to empty my mind a bit so I could sleep; it was still difficult for people to grasp the enormity of the mountain until it was experienced in person. Once Rhian and Cath saw it I think they were both shocked, although they both politely tried not to show it.

My plan was to start with getting a bed ready for Imelda to come home. The three mattresses and bed frame previously in my old bedroom had now gone as they were full of moths and dust and heaven only knows what else. One was so badly decayed it collapsed with shock as we put it in the car and another was full of horsehair. Either I had to go and buy a new single bed or clear a space around the double he already had in his room. It also seemed somewhat counter-productive to go and buy a new bed when he already had one. As I needed to clear Imelda's bedroom anyway, we started there.

I'd warned the girls not to come dressed all "glamour-chick" as the dust had a habit of getting everywhere. After a few minutes in the house the musty, dusty smell covered anyone and everyone inside. The Ikea bags were again invaluable as they were filled up and carried downstairs full of junk to be emptied on the lawn for sorting.

There were piles of old newspapers disintegrating on the floor, in the middle I found a special edition of "*Star Weekly*" dated 1939, a Canadian paper celebrating the royal visit to Canada of the Queen Mother and Princesses Elizabeth and Margaret. I also found a very old pair of round glasses with curly ears, still in their case. At a guess they dated back to the late 1800s.

Other finds in that room included my Christening bracelet and a few other items from when I was a baby.

Cath found a few five pound notes scrunched up on the floor. I stashed them with the others. They'd have been handy for a new bed if we hadn't been able to clear his room in time for him to come home. There were also about nine tins of Ambrosia creamed rice in the bedroom with an expiry date for the following year. I wasn't sure if the thing which was most amazing was that he kept Ambrosia in the bedroom or that the tins were in date.

Two years ago Imelda went on holiday to Benidorm and bought some Spanish Flamenco shoes intended for my twin girls. He got home and told me he'd bought them, only there was a small problem in that somehow he had managed to buy *a pair* with one shoe in a size 22 and the other a 23. He asked me if possibly they might be OK ~ he suggested perhaps a bit of tissue paper could be put in the toe of the larger one. I guess that *may* have been an extreme option for an hour or so for dressing up purposes ~ except he had "misplaced" the shoes and so the girls had to make do with a box of Cadbury's Roses for Christmas. He also failed to notice both were left shoes. Someone saw him coming! We found the shoes during the clear out of his bedroom, now four sizes too small.

We also found *more* of Imelda's own shoes ~ about thirteen shoes this time, twelve of which were paired, brand new and unworn, in boxes.

The girls came outside for some air as the dust was making them sneeze and getting in their eyes. I fetched the box of *new* dust masks I had found a few days before at base camp, but the elastic had totally disintegrated and so they were useless.

I loaded Oggy full of bags again. I thought the poor car could almost have auto piloted herself to the skip she'd been there so often.

While I was at the skip the health assessor rang. She said the medical consultants had started asking why Dad couldn't be sent home. I suggested she show them some photos. She said she *knew* I was working hard but they needed a date when the house would be ready. Um ~ perhaps ten years next Thursday? She said the carpet fitted to the stairs had to be removed as it was threadbare and dangerous. She said wooden stairs were preferable. Ideally he could have agreed to have the rolled one fitted to the stairs ~ killing two birds with one stone. I tried to get her to suggest this to him even though I wasn't sure whether that idea would work.

There also needed to be enough room for him to move about and also any helpers who might need to come into the house. The assessor also said he was likely to need help bathing. Ewwwww! I am his daughter, yes ~ but there are some things I wasn't prepared to do and bathing him was one of them.

She told me she was amazed at his confidence in my ability to do everything for him, to go to his house in the morning to put on his brace and then go back to take it off in the evening plus cooking and whatever else he needed. This was on top of looking after my family with three small children and working 25 hours a week in my job. Any hope of re-starting my college carpentry course the next week was fading rapidly.

I was told they could get him a home help to do some of these things. I'd also been warned that I should get all the help he would need from the outset as professional help could be decreased but it was very difficult to get it increased after release from hospital.

The health assessor asked if I knew anyone who might offer to look after him at their house for a few weeks until his house was ready. I told her I didn't know any saints. She promised she'd call me again the following Monday.

I was finding it difficult to be in the house by that time, not just physically but mentally. I had to escape the mess because I could never relax in surroundings like that. My own kids at home were messy but their mess was just kids' mess ~ only there as the kids were too busy doing kids' stuff which should never be discouraged. None of the kids' mess was there for long ~ they'd always pick it up and put it somewhere else. It may have driven me scatty but I knew, given an hour or so, I could have everything ship shape and smelling of roses again.

Imelda's house, however, was a different matter entirely. Plastic bags had been there so long they'd disintegrated ~ the same plastic bags the Welsh government had banned shops from giving away free because they take so long to decompose... There were still things in that house I'd broken, grown tired of and discarded when I was a teenager. There they remained in the various strata of junk corresponding to the year I threw them out. Shoes I had when I was six reappeared along with a bottle of hand cream I threw out because I didn't like the smell, a pair of tights which had a hole in, a beret which went out of fashion and some shoes I tried to dye but went purple instead of black. I found a Christmas card from my pen pal in Sweden, my old school exercise books, a broken ornament, my school socks and so much more.

I knew I'd thrown them out ~ yet here they all were, still in the house, so now I was throwing them out for the second time. The reason I went to the skip every day was to make absolutely sure that this time, everything was truly gone. I felt smugly satisfied at hearing the bags flop, squelch or crunch as I threw each one over the edge of a skip. It was a spirit-lightening and cleansing feeling.

If I'd had to live in that house with all the junk, not being able to throw anything out because if I did he'd retrieve whatever it was and return it to the house, I would have lost my mental marbles completely. How could anyone relax, live and be happy, in that chaos? I'm sure it was at least a contributing factor to Mum's illness. I became frustrated, headachy and claustrophobic after spending more than an hour at a time there. It was like a nightmare or horror film: I felt the house was eating me alive, the walls were caving in and black stuff oozed out of cupboards. However much stuff I threw out, there was more and more stuff appearing as I progressed through the layers: stuff I knew I'd thrown out years ago was coming back to haunt me. Reality was blurring into a living nightmare.

The houses on either side of Imelda's house were identical to his house in design and size. Both were well maintained stunning looking houses and both were very tidy. I would have *loved* to live in either of them. My friends who came to help all commented what a lovely house it was but what a shame that it had ended up in such a condition. I knew it could become gorgeous again one day but clearly not in the foreseeable future. It was odd, I thought, how, despite the chaos inside the house, Imelda's garden was the best, the most beautifully maintained, the most pristine and manicured of the three. It could almost have been on the cover of a garden magazine.

That night I went to bed hoping not to have nightmares about people-eating houses. I relaxed in the bath with some tasty chocolate liqueurs that my lovely cousin Tanith had sent me. It was one of those unexpected gestures which mean a lot.

# Chapter 15

My truly wonderful mate Jackie and her fabulous husband Mark came down again from Swindon for the day to help me at base camp. I'd put in up a silent prayer for some dry weather for the whole weekend. If only the weather cooperated, I'd try to be a nice daughter to Imelda at visiting time that day. The forecast, however, was rain and it had been raining all night. If the rain kept up I wouldn't be able to do anything because I couldn't go inside the house. Up until then there must have been an angel watching over me because the weather had been dry each time I was there, and as I'd been there between five and eight hours almost every day for the past few weeks, I felt blessed. I often wondered if this was a special angel, if it was, then I suspected I knew her identity.

We arrived at the mountain for an early start. The health assessor had specified that there had to be a clear space around the bed for a health worker to get in and put Imelda's brace on him, so we decided to start there. The floor hadn't been visible for fifteen to twenty years and no one could have stood safely anywhere near the bed.

Jackie and Mark filled bags, carried them downstairs, emptied them on a groundsheet and went back in for more. I sat on the lawn wearing my coat because it was freezing cold, though thankfully dry. I began to sort stuff so dusty that I even had to wear an industrial dust mask outside. Horrible, sticky, thick balls of dust got everywhere. The nasty, musty and dusty smell which I've come to associate with that house got right up my nose despite my mask and I sneezed so much that the neighbour behind next-door's hedge shouted "Bless you!". I spent all day sneezing and wheezing. My eyes were itching and watering but still we ploughed on.

Jackie came out at lunchtime and we had a nice long catch up chat sitting on the lawn sorting through stuff. It was good talking about the old times when we were both kids living in the street.

I found evidence from the bedroom which led me to wonder whether perhaps I'd been adopted; it was a large box of Thornton's chocolates *four* years old. How was that even possible? How could any sane person, let alone anyone related to me, ever leave a box of chocolates unopened for that long? In my house that type of behaviour was unheard of. It had to be a sign of a psychological disorder.

It was amazing to see other things he'd kept that turned up that day. Travel itineraries from years back; all the tickets and paperwork from *all* our family holidays; dozens of leaflets and blank postcards from Benidorm and lots of paper napkins and tissues from everywhere stuffed into every bag and box. There was junk mail and dozens of individually wrapped boiled sweets, that had decomposed/melted through their wrappers making everything sticky ~ all of which, I suspected, must have been given away free at some point.

There must have been hundreds of toothpicks in individual wrappers; for a chap who only had about seven teeth in his head, it was absurd. Scrunched up tissues littered the floor together with receipts from anything and everything he'd ever bought. Each one had to be individually checked because inside six signed visa receipts, neatly folded and with no indication that there was anything of value inside, were three twenty-pound notes, a ten and six fives; some of the fives were the old type that aren't in circulation any longer. More money lurked at the bottom of a crumpled carrier bag with a (used) tissue, odd coins and a couple of toothpicks for company. It had all been there for the previous twenty years or so.

More, odd, but brand new shoes surfaced ~ at a guess and without exaggeration, we'd uncovered about fifty new pairs by then. There were lots of old photographs, another of my mother's diaries from when I was small, an odd shoe belonging to her; two sewing kits, hundreds of daily newspapers dating back to at least 1984; half of them not even opened; lots of junk mail still in plastic mail wrappers; twelve Hawaiian shirts and five pairs of silky pyjama bottoms. We found three unopened packs of new bed sheets ~ odd, because the sheets on his bed which looked as if they had been there years, were threadbare and filthy. There were yet more disintegrated carrier bags, a few of which had a sort of nibbled-on appearance, though I figured it was best not to dwell on that part. Even outside on the lawn there was *so much dust.* It got in my throat, my eyes, my hair and it lingered everywhere. We found more piles of empty envelopes and folded plastic bags.

Midway through the afternoon Ant and his friend Paul, who'd been shopping in town, turned up to help. After ten solid hours with five of us working, the house was greatly improved. We had to stop bringing more stuff out at that point as time, energy, enthusiasm and oxygen had all run out, and besides, we still had to rip the ancient, threadbare carpet off the stairs to make them safe.

Before ripping the fitted carpet up, we had to move the carpet which had lain on the stairs, still rolled up in the same position it had been since it came into the house as a new carpet intended for Imelda's bedroom in 1974. Mark managed to lift it up and *CRACK*, clouds of dust everywhere. The thing virtually disintegrated at the ends where it had become threadbare. The rubber backing had solidified and when it was moved it cracked. Even so I knew Imelda would freak out if we had thrown it out so I asked Mark to put it, folded in half, into my old bedroom.

Mark then got stuck in to the job of pulling the fitted carpet up; together with the grippers it was out in under an hour and loaded into Oggy for a one-way trip to the dump.

'You've squeezed a lot in the car today,' the little skip man said.

'Small car ~ big appetite,' I said ~ a bit like me, really! I'd lost about half a stone in the last four weeks and could have eaten a horse. Some days I got so stuck in to whatever I was doing that I forgot to eat, simple as that. I knew it wasn't healthy and I wasn't trying to diet, merely forgetful.

We got home at 7pm and I went straight to visit Imelda in the hospital. We got to the ward and he was sitting in a chair.

He said, 'I was just thinking nobody had come to visit me for three days'. Bad start Imelda. I'd visited him on Thursday and now it was Saturday. I told him as much.

He dismissed my comment and said, 'Oh well ~ you're here now! Did you bring Ant?'

I pointed out that Ant was an adult and he hadn't wanted to come. I also mentioned, just in passing, that I'd been at the house from 8:30 until 6:30 that day and had only just managed to go home for a shower and a sandwich. I wasn't, therefore, able to collect Ant. My comment was ignored.

I'd had to take all three of the kids with me to the hospital because of my husband's work pattern. The kids didn't like being there, and I spent most of my time nagging them to sit still and stop running around. Kids don't *like* sitting still and my kids are particularly bad at it. They discovered a wheeled stool on the ward for visitors and decided it would make an excellent go-kart... I got increasingly stressed, though Imelda himself was oblivious to the kids' antics. On Imelda's ward were some very sick people and I didn't want my kids to upset them.

A hospital ward isn't the ideal place for small children but I'd had no choice but to take them with me.

I sat on the bed. I was so exhausted by then with the mountain, the kids, the job and the hospital visits that I had absolutely nothing left to say to him. Actually, most of the time I have nothing to say to him, mainly because he apparently has no interest whatsoever in my life. If ever I tried to tell him something that I'd been doing he'd change the subject, dismiss it ~ and me ~ with a flippant, "Oh yes". Sometimes, it simply took too much effort to put everything into very loud and clear monosyllables due to his apparent deafness and stubborn refusal to get a new hearing aid. Communication sometimes seemed a little bit pointless.

The kids were bored and playing up, whizzing themselves around on the wheelie stool. I tried to stop them so many times. Imelda didn't even see how wound up I was getting. The kids tried to talk to him but as he can't hear them he has little idea of what interests them. For the same reason they also have little interest in him and so they carried on playing up. I sat in stressed silence.

He asked how it was going. I told him I was really tired because I'd been at his house for the past three weeks for between four and eight hours a day, almost every day. I waited for a reaction.

'Right,' he said.

I told him we'd tackled the stair-carpet that day and had taken it away because the health assessor had said it was so frayed it was dangerous. I told him what a nasty job it had been, with dust flying everywhere and the rubber underlay getting everywhere because it had totally disintegrated. I said I'd had to go outside while Mark did this because of my rubber and dust allergies, but I'd still been wheezing and asthmatic because it had affected my lungs.

'Did you try to pull it off in one piece as I suggested?' he asked, 'so we can measure it for the new one.'

I pointed out that that would have been impossible. The bloody thing had disintegrated to such an extent it had come off in about 27 trillion pieces. I also proudly mentioned that we'd cleared a big space next to his bed, and the bedroom itself should be finished within the week. Did he thank me? Did he heck!

'When I get out I'll need help with the netting in the garden!' he said. 'I need to prune the fruit bushes because I've worked so hard to make them bear fruit and they have been doing so well.'

Determined to make him to show at least *some* appreciation, I told him we'd found lots of old-type five pound notes in bags on his floor. I expected amused surprise, possibly gratitude.

'And you probably found lots of old stamps there too,' he said irritably, 'but you don't throw *them* out!' What? ~ I realised afterwards he was assuming I was asking him about the five pound notes because I wanted to throw them out. Did he truly think I was that stupid? Quite clearly he did.

I'd been there about 45 minutes and decided it was time to go: the kids were bored stupid and I could feel my anger and frustration just coming to the boil.

When I got home I relaxed on my sofa and browsed my laptop for hoarder websites. There were a surprising number and it was good to realise I wasn't the only one who had to go through something like this. There were forums and other web sites for hoarders. I wasn't alone.

# Chapter 16

Four weeks had passed since Imelda fell off his ladder and he was still in hospital. He had been fitted with a back brace and thankfully was still able to walk albeit very painfully. His days involved intensive physiotherapy and a lot of rest.

My days now included almost daily visits to the house, then the recycling centre with my car stuffed full of junk, and then to visit Imelda in hospital. I rushed from bill-paying and getting statements at the bank to the optician to sort out his glasses, made countless calls to various friends and relatives of his, and went to the church to get his newsletter. Despite wearing a dust mask every time I visited the house, I still had a permanent blocked, runny nose, itchy eyes and a wheezy chest.

Many of my amazing friends had travelled some distance to come and help me and had even taken days off work. Despite all the time and effort, in my view the house didn't look much different from when we'd started, although the walkways between rooms were wider and there was now some space around his bed. The kitchen table was now visible and two of the rooms had been cleared and re-filled, though to anyone seeing the house for the first time it would still register as a horrendously cluttered house.

After all those weeks of house sorting, working four evenings a week and trying to entertain three young children, I was totally exhausted. I was also horribly aware that I was due to start year two of my carpentry course at college the following week.

On one side I was being nagged by Imelda not to throw anything out: on the other I was being nagged by the social workers to get things sorted so that he could come home. It was impossible to sort out the house without throwing stuff out. Some of his things had to go ~ there simply was no other way, though his opinion was that I could just tidy up. To tidy, one needs a place to store stuff: all his stores were full to overflowing. Imelda seemed completely oblivious to the real situation and was getting angrier and angrier with me and I still hadn't had a single word of thanks or even appreciation.

My friends were very supportive, and were all, without exception, of the opinion I should have just told him to let me clear it. They said I should ask him whether he trusted me enough to decide what had to go out ~ or I left him in the hospital. It was his choice.

Early one morning Imelda rang me from the hospital. He said he hadn't slept because he was concerned about three things he was afraid I might have thrown out. One of them, I hadn't; one, I might have; the third lay at the bottom of a skip somewhere in Cardiff. Heck!

He mentioned letters regarding certain financial issues ~ these I hadn't even seen, though I knew I hadn't thrown away anything financial from the previous three years. I'd sorted paperwork carefully: any letters over six years old were out of date for tax purposes or for anything else, so they were discarded. I felt it was a bit unfair for him to mention these concerns four full weeks after he knew I had started clearing.

I was beginning to feel the stress. The more time I spent in that house the more I was convinced that the whole thing was totally futile. I so wanted to get that house looking good again: cleared and tidy as it had once been, but every day the house fought back. Every minor triumph ~ clearing a space so that a door could open properly was immediately negated because that door was part of an untidy, completely dysfunctional room that was just one small part of a whole house in total chaos. Clearing one kitchen cupboard, which should have been a small triumph, never was, because after spending a couple of hours clearing and cleaning each shelf, I then had to find a place to put everything that had come out ~

and which was now occupying most of the space I had cleared and celebrated the day before!

When I cleared a cupboard I *tried* to see it as a step forward ~ but I'd then remember that it was only one cupboard in a kitchen with twelve cupboards. The floor level cupboards had to have an area in front cleared before I could open the doors and reach the contents. Each cupboard was a single step towards the finish line ~ and I was in reverse gear while the finish line was heading for the hills.

~

I realised I was showing signs of cracking up when I cried at an episode of EastEnders and three days later howled over a TV advert that wasn't even a sad one! I knew things weren't right when, watching a dog adventure story for kids, *"The Littlest Hobo"* one Saturday morning, I found myself bawling my eyes out at the end. I've never been an emotional type apart from when I was expecting our twins ~ which I'd say was excusable! Yet, a month at the mountain and I was crying at the drop of a hat. I felt life was so unfair: I hadn't asked for this; I hadn't ever contributed to the mess ~ yet here was I being forced to deal with it by circumstances beyond my control.

I found myself, often, thinking about my poor mother, who had hated the mess as much as I did ~ probably much more ~ yet she'd had to live there every day. In her diaries she described it as "a mountain of insurmountable junk".

She, like me, also suffered from asthma yet couldn't vacuum because of the decreasing area of visible carpet. She enjoyed polishing our big mahogany dining table with fragrant wood polish, but to do this she'd have to move piles of paperwork first ~ and then put them back afterwards. She loved to cook but to do this properly she needed working space in the kitchen, and the available space in that kitchen shrank daily.

Mum made pretty dresses for me when I was a little girl but wasn't ever allowed to clear the table to do it ~ she had to move the papers aside to make room for the sewing machine. The papers gathered dust, of course, but she couldn't vacuum or dust papers! My friends, when I brought them home, used to ask me why my mother sneezed so often ~ summer evenings, with the windows open, they could hear her sneezing from their houses a few doors away!

I'd begun to hate the sight of the house. Resentment and loathing overcame me as I turned the corner and saw it at the end of the street. I got a bitter taste in my mouth and my stomach fell even when I talked about it. Like a rotting apple the house looked fine from outside but, opened up, it was obviously bad. I'd called this place 'home'. It had become 'hell'.

At this point I went on strike and took a day off. It was getting too much. Right then, I was even looking forward to work, which became an oasis of normality in my surreal life.

The anniversary of my mother's passing came four weeks after Imelda's accident. I remembered it despite the fact that it was an incredibly busy day. As well as everything else, I started year two of the carpentry course at college.

We had a talk from the college staff: we couldn't be late; how to fill in grant application forms and we had to have at least 90% attendance. We weren't allowed to start late or leave early because we had to become accustomed to work ethics. It was assumed that nobody on the course had ever had a job because most of the students were teenage boys straight from school.

There were two routes in the carpentry course for year two, bench joinery or site carpentry. Bench joinery was in the warm workshop, paying attention to detail and using all the power tools. Site work was on site in the cold and wet, often high up. It also involved lugging heavy materials about. It was very physical work and the ideal worker was a big, beefy, young bloke. I was neither big, beefy nor young and I was most definitely not a bloke. Yet for some reason I had been put down for site carpentry...

I cornered the tutor at break for a quick chat. I told him I was sorry, but I'd have to prove the exception to all his rules. I'd be late every day because I had three kids to take to school as well as some temporary problems. I wasn't interested in work ethics either ~ I was the only one on the course with a job and I'd been almost permanently employed since I left school thirty years or so before. I'd also, I told him, be leaving early most days to go to work. I wasn't going to bother staying for two hours after lunch that day to waste time filling in a twenty page grant form either ~ I was the only one who didn't qualify for a grant. I was also willing to pay for my own rubbery beans and chips in the student canteen at lunch time.

While the tutor spluttered I pointed out that this was how it had been last year, and I'd passed that with a distinction. There wasn't much he could say to that ~ other than he was grateful I hadn't said it in front of the class!

I'd hoped I'd be in the same class as the girls from last year's course: there had been only three of us in a class of about twenty. The rest had been bollock-scratching teenage boys who communicated only with grunts and until they joined the human race then I didn't want to mix with them.

Once we'd all completed the initial assessments we were allowed home at lunchtime. I rode home on my motorbike ~ the first time I'd ridden it for a month. I changed, grabbed a banana and a Kit Kat, jumped in Oggy and headed for the mountain.

I got there at 1:00, opened the door and was almost bowled over by the dog in need of an obviously urgent wee on the grass. At this point I realised he had a dodgy tummy and was trying to wipe off a cling-on. I took the Ikea bags inside and got stuck in and found another five shoes to add to the shoe pile. Imelda indeed! I'd thought *my* boot collection was excessive! Within half an hour I'd found seven more shoes: I flexed one and the sole, brittle with age, snapped. He'd actually had one odd shoe repaired; I wondered why when he had so many!

There were hundreds of paper napkins all either used or scrunched up and I filled eleven green bags with them and old newspapers from 1996. I found share certificates for companies I'd never heard of. Also there were thirteen odd socks, three woolly hats, a pair of scraggy underpants, lots of coins from 1p to £2 and a few shillings and pesetas together with two ten franc notes and a book of first class stamps. There was so much dust I was doing thirteen sneezes in a row, despite wearing a full industrial dust mask.

Miraculously, the rain held off and the sun came out so I could sort in the garden, yet it had poured that morning and rain had been forecast for the whole day. I was beginning to believe someone was looking after me; friends volunteered help exactly when I needed it most; the weather stayed fine while I sorted despite terrible forecasts and often the sun shone too. I couldn't believe the run of luck I was having with the weather. I also, suddenly, had a strong sense of determination. This situation wouldn't beat me although it would have beaten many people. I believed that my mother, my Guardian Angel, had something to do with it!

At 6:30 I had to leave because the skip closed at 6:45. I filled Oggy with thirteen green bags, bits of wood, broken plant pots, an old beige hand basin, jars of some sort of paint, boxes, old bottles, dusty plastic souvenirs, three tatty shoes and an old wooden stool. I got to the skip, parked up, and little skip man appeared and asked if I wanted a hand. I politely declined ~ I enjoyed lobbing a full bag over the edge of the skip and watching it disappear for ever and hearing the satisfying crash when it hit the bottom.

Little skip man said, 'You've been working hard, haven't you?' I explained the situation. He'd seen programmes about hoarders on television and thought they were set up. Sadly not, they were real. I carried on throwing bags into the skip and he helped me with the sink. It crashed into the bottom of the skip. We both smiled.

'See you soon,' I said.

'No doubt,' he smiled.

At home I grabbed a bite to eat, had a quick wash and then went to the hospital for the evening visit. Imelda was sitting up in bed, very cross because the health assessor hadn't been to see him yet. I got the impression he didn't like her because of her no-nonsense approach. She told him straight! He wanted to know what the hell the hold-up was. He repeated that he couldn't possibly sort things out while he was incarcerated in hospital. He appeared to be under the impression he'd be released within two days: I wasn't going to argue with him but it seemed unlikely. He didn't seem to think that five foot walls of junk were an issue. This was going to be interesting. He had another whinge about being stuck in the hospital and I considered reminding him that it was hospital, not jail ~ but then thought better of it. I didn't want to put ideas into his head. Instead, I mentioned that I'd been in the house for five hours that day.

He said, 'Yes, I know you've been there a lot.'

'I'm absolutely worn out, Dad. I've been working so hard.'

He didn't reply to that. No sympathy, no "I understand", not even a "How's it going?" and definitely, positively, no thanks at all.

'A doctor, some *female*, came to see my ears today,' he said. 'She gave me some drops.' I gritted my teeth when he called her "some female". I knew no one else, at all, who ever used this term about a fellow human. Most people would say, "a lady doctor" or even "a woman doctor", but never, ever "some female". It was bloody sexist and it annoyed the hell out of me.

After an hour I decided it was time to go. He didn't thank me for coming, or for bringing the post, or cleaning the house or being the daughter he felt he was entitled to have. He asked me to phone after the health assessor had called. I told him she would update him and got up to leave. Again, hoping for the sympathy vote or at least a word of thanks for my six hours graft that day, I tried to look as knackered as I could and let out a huge sigh ~ a performance worthy of an Oscar! Unfortunately, it went straight over his head.

'Will you be in tomorrow?' he asked, hopefully.

'No Dad ~ I've got college all day and work in the evening!'

'Oh yes,' he said, 'so can I phone you when you get home in the evening?'

'No Dad. I don't finish until eleven so don't phone.' This was a lie, I finished work at 9:30 and if he'd ever listened to me he'd have known this, but he didn't. I just didn't want to speak to him after work.

I smiled to myself at my mate's suggestion of a solution to this whole mess. 'Get him a bigger ladder for his birthday.' she said. It was a thought!

I didn't anticipate things getting any easier for me any time in the near future. I was getting regular headaches ~ unusual for me. As well as my blocked and runny nose my skin was dry and itchy. Despite being exhausted, I couldn't sleep, so I was getting snappy with the kids. It was also getting more difficult to be polite to the customers whinging at me in work often about the most trivial issues. The mountain wasn't much smaller and I was barely out of base camp. Work became a calm port amid the storm. I felt obliged to make hospital visits at least every second day and the hospital and social services were pestering me daily about when the house would be ready for Imelda to come home.

It felt as if I was being chased by an avalanche: I was constantly rushing from A to B to C and back again (via the skip). The kids complained I never had time to read with them. They said things like, "Aw mum, you're not working *again* are you?" or "You're not going to Granddad's house *again* are you?"

I arrived at college on day two at 10:00. Everyone else had started at 9:00. Because I'd explained my problems to the college staff, my lateness wasn't a problem, but everybody else had seen the day's demonstration and were engrossed in drawing a rod to make a sash window. The tutor showed me what to do but I was aware that he'd have had to do this twice, once for the main class and then again for me and I was always going to get the rushed version. I'd also miss out at the end of sessions on days when I had to go to work. I don't work fixed days, so it was likely to be different days every week. Trying to get my company to work around me, or even fix my days in work had historically proved a long and arduous task.

At morning break I sat for twenty minutes amongst the grunting, bollock scratchers. The break was a complete waste of time when I could have been doing something worthwhile. Lunch time wasted another hour: I contemplated attempting to translate the grunts into intelligent conversation but soon gave up. I discussed my thoughts with my mate Sian over lunch, just needing to untangle my thoughts. I was grateful to her for listening to me, because when I'd verbalised my thoughts I realised I couldn't give proper concentration or commitment to college with so much else going on. Sadly, college, the bottom of my list of current priorities, would suffer, and if I left now then someone else could still take my place.

I had a word with the tutor who was very understanding and helpful. He said he didn't want to lose me: I was a good student and a hard worker and they needed more students like me, he said, and anything else he could think of to make me reconsider and stay. The college had noted my 97% attendance last year, and was happy for me to take time off. I wasn't used to people being sympathetic listeners and with my emotional state at the time I ended up howling my head off and being sent home to have a think about my options. As I saw it I had no options.

Ant phoned that evening. He'd visited Imelda earlier in the day. I hadn't: I didn't think my frayed nerves could stand it without snapping, and that wouldn't have been pretty. He'd asked Imelda why he thought the house was still a mess when he had been retired for twenty years. Imelda said it was because he did too much! Luckily he didn't say that to me! Apparently he was worrying more about the "idiot" who lived across the garden hedge who was hell bent on cutting the hedge to a level where he could see through the garden to the rather nice view from the front of Imelda's house.

However, the hedge had a preservation order on it and nobody was allowed to cut it without permission, as the *idiot* was aware, having been so informed by the City Council. The hedge had been about 20-30ft high for as long as I could remember, but the neighbour had been cutting it bit by bit ~ usually when Imelda was in church, and had been having a field day since Imelda had been in hospital. In one place it was now only six feet high.

Imelda wasn't happy to hear this and vowed to involve the police when he got out. Personally, I thought perhaps Imelda's priorities needed rearranging and there were more important things to worry about ~ the health assessor was due at the house the next day to see my progress so it would be another full day at the mountain.

That evening I went to a friend's 40th birthday bash, taking two of the five pound notes I'd found at the house. I was keeping count of all the money I'd found, intending to present him with a lump sum when he came home. I handed one of the fives over to pay for my drink.

In front of everyone in the bar the barmaid shouted, 'We can't take this, it's too colourful.' I offered her the other one. She checked it in the ultra violet machine and refused that too. They both had a silver line and a watermark but had apparently been in the house so long that they were no longer in circulation ~ or they were forgeries and had been palmed off on an old man. She suggested I took the notes to the bank, but if I had and they were dodgy, the bank would have kept them and I'd have been £10 down as well as possibly being locked up for passing counterfeit money! Luckily my friend bailed me out at the bar...

I was at base camp early the next day, determined to sort the house out for the health assessor's return visit that afternoon. In the bedroom I managed to clear all around the bed and make it safe ~ I could even see the original wooden floorboards, which developed a loud creak that day. Not a nasty pressure creak, more a creak of relief! How they hadn't snapped under the weight over the years, I don't know. If floorboards could party, then that's what they would have done that night!

# Chapter 17

The health assessor arrived and told me I was amazing and had done wonders. I was thrilled to hear that even though the house was still a shocking mess. But ~ had I done enough for Imelda to come home?

She took herself on a quick tour of the house and I followed. In my opinion it still looked as if nothing had changed, in places the junk was still up to four feet high. Would I ever be free of this place?

'So we'll make arrangements for your dad to be released.' Her voice jabbed into my subconscious.

That was it then, he was finally coming home. Imelda had apparently persuaded the health assessors and social workers that the second he got home he'd start sorting the mess, though I thought it was more likely he'd driven the hospital staff insane and they couldn't get shot of him quickly enough.

Before he came home, social services needed to fit a hand rail on one side of the stairs, fix the toilet flush and carry out a few other small jobs. The health assessor left a bulky big white plastic seat attached to the toilet, very kindly taking the box it came in away with her. She said she'd usually have left it but in this case she thought I'd appreciate her taking it.

~

I had to step things up a level to get everything finished before he left hospital. I knew he'd never allow me to carry on clearing once he was home. I whizzed round the house like a woman possessed, picking up anything which was clearly rubbish. I filled bags with eleven shoes, eight vile Hawaiian shirts, lots of old man's underpants, bags of my clothes I'd thrown out when I was eighteen, odd socks, lots and lots of old newspapers, two broken clocks, old coat hangers, more toothpicks, some old tin labels, holiday itineraries and tickets dating back to 1996, more of my mum's tights, empty boxes and bits of total rubbish. To my horror about two feet from the top of a pile was a very swish large box of chocolates still in the cellophane wrapper and tied in a huge yellow ribbon. There was no date on the box, nor was there a bar code. What a tragic waste. I estimated they were at least twenty years old. Not even I would risk twenty year old chocolates! I also found five bags of fruit pastilles dated April 2001 ~ they'd solidified.

I sorted twelve bags full of paper recycling and a black bin bag of rubbish. I also filled the neighbours' bins as it was bin collection day and they'd assured me they didn't mind. I emptied both of Imelda's council wheelie bins of the wood he had stored in them and filled them both in under an hour. Bin collection day also gave Oggy a day off from the skip run ~ I hoped the guys at the skip didn't worry about me. I stayed until the bin men had been, wanting to make sure they didn't leave a single thing for Imelda to take back inside.

I decided to go and buy a shoe rack and a clothes rail for Imelda. He could keep thirty pairs on a rack and the rest could go to charity. I planned to get the kids involved on a "sort the shoe" mission, telling them it was a real life version of the game "pairs".

As I left Imelda's house that day the rain began and by the time I got home it was pouring. This weather quirk no longer surprised me. Had it rained earlier, I'd have been forced to either abandon ship entirely or attempt to clear up inside which would have been foolish with my dust allergies. My Guardian Angel had been watching out for me again!

If anything more was going to be thrown out it had to go before Imelda arrived home or it would stay in there forever. When he got home I'd have to be far more subtle about sorting his stuff. I knew he wouldn't let me touch, let alone sort or ~ heaven forbid! ~ dispose of stuff. He'd expressed surprise one day when I told him I'd taken some old rags to the skip. His actual words were, "Oh so you have found a skip somewhere have you?"

That was one way of putting it! I'd found an enormous skip, free to residents, at the council recycling centre. "Free" was a word that usually made Imelda sit up and take notice, but he obviously wasn't listening.

I took all three kids to visit Imelda that night. When I arrived he was sitting up in bed.

'Oh, there you are,' he said. 'I've been trying to contact you for the past two hours but I keep getting a strange tone.' This, clearly, was entirely my fault!

'There's nothing wrong with my phone that I know of,' I said, 'we've had calls today no problem.'

'Well I tried about eight times ~ one of the kids must have been on the computer.' He said this every time he called and my telephone was engaged. Each time I had to explain to him in words of one syllable that it did not matter if 73 people were on a PC in my house because the telephone line was separate from the computer. For continuity and for the benefit of my health, I explained yet again.

He looked at me blankly. 'Well, someone must've been on the computer because I couldn't get through.'

I asked what number he'd called and he showed me the phone display ~ which was one digit out. Naturally, this was my also my fault. We finally established that had he used the number that corresponded to the telephone in my house he'd have had a better chance of reaching me.

The kids were bored stiff, playing up and trying to push each other round the ward on the wheelie stool. The ward was full of visitors and the kids were on full form. Imelda did not appear to notice and within minutes of me arriving he picked up the phone to call Ant. I sat on his bed like a lemon while he rang (rudely, I thought) and had a chat with Ant. Finally the kids got so bad I decided it was time to go. He saw me stand up and finished the call. I asked why he'd phoned Ant while the kids and I were there visiting him and not waited until we'd gone.

His response was that he was "trying to get the family to communicate with each other," as if he were the kingpin, and only he was keeping the family together, clearly of the opinion that we wouldn't or couldn't do this without him. I reminded him that Ant and I had spoken to each other at least once a day, every day, on the phone as well as all the time we spent together at the house.

He said, 'Well I don't know that do I?'

I felt like saying 'Well you ****ing would if you bothered listening,' but I didn't, because by this time he was having a go at me because nobody had told him when he was going home. I told him the health assessor had said he could go home soon. He decided this meant that he'd be going home the following day and asked me to buy bread and milk and some pineapple chunks on my way over to the mountain.

I agreed, ~ it wasn't a problem ~ until he asked if I needed him to write it down for me.

I turned to go and the kids raced off down the corridor. They knew their granddad would want to kiss them goodbye and none of them were daft enough to hang around that long. They'd all disappeared before he even stood up.

I returned from that night's hospital visit wondering why I bothered visiting when I came home so wound up.

I still didn't know exactly when he'd be released. On one hand the hospital had been calling to find out when the house would be ready for him, but on the other, the ward staff, oddly, didn't seem to be in a rush to release him. If he'd been treating the nurses the same way he'd been treating me, he'd have been out head first!

The sister from Imelda's ward called me the following morning. She said, in my opinion trying to hide the relief in her voice just a teeny bit too hard, that

Imelda could come home that day. Whatever reaction she expected from me, I was pretty sure it wasn't the expression of horror that she got.

The whole house was still upside down, rather like those little games kids had where small tiles in a small, flat frame had to be slid around to put numbers in order. To move one square it was necessary to move most of the others first, one at a time. Clearing a hoarder's house was like that ~ only without the single space. One pile of stuff has to be moved in order to get another pile of stuff out so that a different pile of stuff could go there.

There were boxes everywhere that all had to be put in their place ~ although where that place actually was, was anybody's guess. They'd been intended as temporary storage in the kitchen until the house was clear, but now had nowhere to go. Nightmare! There was a "last ditch, now or never" atmosphere. Ant and I ran around like idiots trying to get as much obvious junk out of the house in as little time as we possibly could.

The situation had become urgent. Oggy was already full of stuff, so we squashed it all down to squeeze even more in. We dragged a broken chair from a pile and had to clear up the resulting avalanche, old clothes, old shoes and lots and lots more old newspapers.

Despite the gigantic efforts made by Ant, my mates and me, if anyone new had visited at that stage they would have been horrified to the core at the appalling mess that remained. I'd done so much work in that house; often returning home totally and utterly knackered and stinking of musty, dusty, unclean junk. Each night I got home and streaked up my stairs to the shower after dumping my clothes downstairs in a sealed bag ready for the following day. I'd totally neglected my poor family and was too tired even to talk to anyone when I came home. I'd made trips at least once daily to the skip and had developed a friendship with the skip men. I'd recycled about nine bags of newspapers every day. There had been days when I had lots of help from my friends and days when I'd been alone all day, just sorting. I had the most amazing suntan from spending so long in the garden (although the minute I left, it rained) and for his financial security I'd filled my barbecue with all the receipts and papers bearing his name and address and burned them. Now, everything was about to change.

~

I'd read books on hoarding in the past and so I knew his behaviour was quite common although I didn't understand how a person could be comfortable living the way he did. I knew that hoarding was classed as a mental illness and that hoarders had an emotional attachment to everything they owned and so found it difficult to throw anything away. Surely though, if someone had 137 wine bottle corks in a carrier bag then the 138th could go in the bin. Apparently not! Perhaps it was like smoking, even though people knew how damaging it was to their health and their wallet, they smelled bad and they knew their health would suffer, they still lit up.

Maybe the happy sense of satisfaction I get from having a major clean and clear up in my own house is a bit extreme ~ possibly brought on by my experiences growing up. I feel cleansed when I throw anything out. I still love the feeling of a clean tidy house with everything in its place and no dust anywhere. I can live with a mess for a while – with three kids, some mess is normal. I also know that I'd never be able to live in the level of mess at Imelda's house and stay sane.

My mother became mentally unstable at a very early age. Back then, I accepted what I was told; I was young and somewhat blinkered. In light of what I had heard from neighbours during the weeks I'd spent at the mountain I had some suspicions that the diagnosis of premature Alzheimer's, a term flung about by one or two medical people at the time, was possibly inaccurate.

Alzheimer's disease was never officially diagnosed. I understood such a diagnosis could only be confirmed by an autopsy; however the death certificate didn't mention it. I didn't have the full medical facts but so many people I knew firmly believed she may have suffered a mental breakdown that I could not discount them all. Did Imelda's hoarding cause it?

# Chapter 18

Mum was only 47 when we noticed that her everyday behaviour wasn't quite right, and it soon became clear to those who knew her well and loved her, that she was beginning to have mental issues. She changed gradually over several years from a gentle, funny, loving and intelligent person into a depressed, confused, angry and violent one. Various doctors suggested her symptoms were similar to early onset Alzheimer's disease. This version of Alzheimer's tends to run in families ~ but there is no history of it in our family as far as we knew.

The first incident I remember was on a family holiday in Spain. I came in to the hotel reception one day to find Mum in the foyer shaking, terrified and crying hysterically, having gone from the poolside to her room to get something, but had mistakenly gone into room 597 instead of her room which was 497: same location wrong floor. She'd been caught in there by the room's occupant who thought she was a burglar, he'd become nasty and grabbed my frightened mother and frogmarched her to reception which was where I found her. By the time I arrived the man had mellowed slightly and other people were trying to calm her down. The man left her with me and I apologised and explained she'd not been quite right recently.

The following day she'd calmed down and almost forgotten the incident. She was sitting under a shady tree writing a postcard to her parents and had written their name on the card but had put our address. She'd also tried to write the address in the box at the top right of the card which was designed for stamps. Little things perhaps, but added together we were becoming worried as we had no idea what was wrong.

Over the following years things got worse. Mum's personality changed and she regularly switched from being her usual cheerful self to somebody who was terrified and convinced my dad was the devil himself.

'I know you don't believe me,' she'd say, 'but he is *evil*'. She'd demand that we get the vicar because she needed to see him and on three occasions we actually had to take her to see the vicar in order to settle her.

A few times she went out for a walk with the two black poodles we had at the time, Holly and Daffny. She left the house with both dogs and returned three hours later with only one, having no recollection that we'd ever had two.

Neighbours reported her often knocking on their doors. She'd go inside and sit down as if she were in her own house. Luckily the neighbours were very understanding.

By the age of about 53 she'd become extremely confused. She was still driving at this point although we were trying to persuade her to stop as it was clearly unsafe. We mentioned it to the doctor who was unable to intervene. She forgot which way she had to move the indicator to turn left or right. I tried so hard to make it simple for her but sometimes the harder I tried to explain things in an attempt to make them simple, the more complicated they appeared to become.

Everyday tasks became difficult; she forgot how to make a cup of tea, she poured milk into the teapot, she forgot which direction the tap turned on and tried for ages to turn it the wrong way in an attempt to get water to come out. She often left the front door open, she forgot to put powder in the washing machine and she left the taps on. The television remote ended up in the fridge and her shoes in the dishwasher.

Her general behaviour became inappropriate. One morning at about 3am Mum decided it was time to get up, get dressed and go out. It was very difficult to stop her as she was convinced she was right and we were wrong. She tried to tuck her skirt into her tights and then put her nightie over her coat. Her slippers became a permanent fixture inside, outside and in bed. She lost all ability to understand money and would give a ten pound note for a loaf of bread and often walk out without the change. When she was given the change she would express extreme gratitude as if the sales assistant was giving her a gift. She would also walk out with items from a shop, totally forgetting that she was meant to pay for them first.

The wandering became a worry: if she went out in the night or when we were asleep, she could try to break in to a neighbour's house. We had to lock the doors in case this happened.

We bought her several safety bracelets and necklaces with her name address and telephone number on in case she wandered but she pulled them off and they were lost.

Ten minutes after eating lunch she would ask "What's for lunch?" having no recollection of having eaten only minutes before. Showing her the evidence of the plates still in the sink didn't convince her she'd already eaten.

As Mum had asthma it was a huge worry that she'd go somewhere, have an attack and not be able to get help. Not only did she lose her inhaler daily but she was losing her coordination and wasn't able to take it by herself. I remembered one occasion when I'd been out with a friend and passed her while coming home in the car. I saw her struggling to make it up the road obviously having trouble breathing. We stopped the car and I asked her if she had her inhaler. After she realised who I was, she was still clearly confused and said she didn't. I asked her to look in her pocket. She eventually found her pocket and put her hand in and took the inhaler out saying there was nothing in her pocket. I pointed out it was now in her hand but she didn't understand and was becoming agitated, as was I.

I told her, 'Mum ~ your inhaler's in your hand!' but still she wasn't able to understand. I reached out of the car to take it from her but she moved her hand away as if I was trying to steal something from her.

'I can't breathe!' she said. Again I tried to take the inhaler from her hand to give it to her but she grabbed my wrist and dug her nails in hard as if I were trying to attack her.

These were just a few of the many incidents that occurred. We had to make sure there was always someone with her just in case something happened. Her behaviour became more and more challenging. Things were made even more difficult as each episode of odd behaviour was interspersed with a period of apparent normality. Each time we went to the doctor she was back to her usual self.

The doctor finally referred her to the memory clinic as she forgot both recent and long term events. She forgot her friends' names and was unable to remember her own address or telephone number. She wasn't able to sign her own name and would write in childlike scrawl. It was difficult to get official documents signed. Eventually Dad and I were granted joint Power of Attorney for her.

Once she went out "for a short walk" before lunch. Three hours later she was still missing. When we finally heard the front door, Ant, evidently extremely relieved, screamed from the back room,

'Where the hell have you been?' He went to the door to find Mum in between two burly police officers who had brought her home as she had been reported wandering around the local park in a confused state.

After a few years we had a social worker involved and Mum was able to go into a residential home for a few days at a time for assessment and as a break for the family. Each time she went into the care home she would stay a bit longer until eventually she was admitted "for the foreseeable future" to the local mental hospital.

It was heart breaking to see her in there. Most of the others in the ward were elderly and many had been diagnosed with Alzheimer's disease. The place was awful, full hopeless despair.

I visited her as often as I could. I couldn't turn and give Mum a hug and a kiss at the end of my visit because if I did she thought I was attacking her and retaliated by trying to scratch my eyes out. Often, when I had finished my visits, Mum and some of the others often followed me out of the day room and down the corridor to the end of the ward where there was a glass door with a security lock. The visitors knew the lock combination but the patients, for their own security, didn't. I had to almost sprint down the corridor to get out of the locked door. After an Olympic effort to get to the door fast, the number had to be remembered and jabbed in accurately and quickly before the ward inmates caught up. I can only describe it as similar to being chased by the zombies from Michael Jackson's "*Thriller*" video! They didn't move fast but they were fast enough and heaven only knows what would have happened had they caught up before I'd got out. What if the lock combination was changed and the lock wouldn't open? The door also had a slow closing mechanism fitted to it to stop people getting their fingers jammed. This was somewhat counter-productive as if it was too slow they would catch up and grab the door. It was a heavy door and most of them were elderly and frail, although surprisingly some were incredibly strong. I was terrified their fingers would get caught and broken. Those fears haunted me for months.

Once the door was closed it was vital to make sure the door had clicked shut to protect the patients from their own desires to get out. Always there were three or four of them who waited all day for the opportunity to escape. I felt truly rotten to the core at having to shut the old ladies in. They would scream to be let out, claw at the glass, rattle the door handle and shake the door. Those moments were very upsetting for me.

As I walked down the long, lonely, echoing corridors of that hospital I felt the atmosphere, thick with the ghosts of past patients. Even on the hottest of summer days it was cold. I always walked quickly, as I could hear the disturbing clawing of glass and howling of the inmates of west four, pleading and crying for me to let them out. Their howls blended into the general ghostly and eerily sad atmosphere of the place.

On more than one occasion I saw a sad old man sitting in the corridor staring into space and rocking. I walked on past, whether he was a patient having been allowed out for a walk or had escaped from one of the wards I didn't know. I feared speaking to him in case he was violent. It was, after all a place of the unknown and the forgotten. He could have been anyone, he could have been someone from another place in time, I didn't know, I never tried to interfere.

Mum eventually forgot how to speak. I was greeted with "Babababababababa baba ba," if she was in a good mood or "Darrrr errr grrrr" if she wasn't. Sometimes she remembered who I was, usually she didn't. Sometimes she screamed like a banshee when I visited and other times she would have to be restrained from attacking Dad when he came to visit alone.

Many patients on the ward would simply be put in a chair first thing in the morning where they would stay, staring into space, dribbling and muttering to themselves all day. The television was always on but I doubt any of them ever understood it. A few occasions I visited when they were watching *Teletubbies*. This was probably deliberate as I don't think they could have understood anything much more advanced. At least it was colourful with a bit of music. Many of the patients spent their time loudly shouting the same phrase over and over,

"Eric it is six o'clock. You have to get the bus. Eric. Eric it's six o'clock"... I learned Eric had passed away in 1952.

The nurses in the hospital were wonderful. The patience and understanding they showed was truly inspiring. Each and every patient would be dressed nicely each day and the nurses would sit and talk to them whenever they had the time.

As her mental health declined, Mum forgot how to clean her teeth so they rotted and were eventually all removed in one hit. She was put in a normal medical hospital for this as it was less traumatic for her to be given a general anaesthetic. I went to see her that night about four hours after the operation. It was heart breaking to see her lying there on the ward. She appeared to have aged drastically overnight. Here was my poor mother totally toothless, confused, drugged, upset, alone and frightened in a place she didn't recognise. The staff had put her in a side ward alone in case her screaming upset the other patients. They'd pulled the sides of the bed up to stop her falling out. It looked as if she were in a cot.

She hadn't been by herself for years, having been in a mental ward which always had many other people in it. Even the bedrooms on the mental ward had eight beds in each and a nurse present at all times. In this regular NHS hospital she was confused. She was obviously in pain from having all her teeth removed, there was blood seeping from her mouth which had dried over her face.

What upset me the most was that they had left the needle in the back of her hand and she was scratching at it to try to get it out. I tried to stop her clawing at herself but then she tried to attack me believing I was trying to hurt her. I asked the nurse to remove it several times over the two hours I was there until eventually I told them I was going to remove it myself as I couldn't bear to see her like that. This got them moving and it took a nurse under a minute to remove it.

It wasn't practical to fit her with false teeth as she would have tried to swallow anything in her mouth or spit it out. Her food had to be mushed up so she didn't choke as she forgot how to chew. Feeding her was painfully slow as she couldn't co-ordinate opening her mouth with the arrival of the food on the spoon. Her food rarely made it to her mouth before it was cold. Occasionally when I was there at meal times I was asked if I'd like to help her with her food. It was difficult; when a mother feeds a baby, she puts the food, of similar consistency, on a spoon and *flies* it towards the baby's mouth, perhaps making aeroplane noises for good measure. The baby then automatically opens its mouth for the food. Mum didn't. It was challenging. When she did open her mouth she'd often close it again too soon, spilling half of the food back down her chin.

On 9th September 1994, I was at work when I had a call from the hospital where Mum had been for about four years. A horrible feeling of unease rushed through my bones the minute I took the call. The nurse asked me if I was OK and at that moment I knew I wasn't.

Apparently Mum had woken during the night at about 2am, sat bolt upright in bed and started chattering away loudly to herself. As she was in a ward of about eight people the nurse went over, held her hand and gently told her she should go back to sleep, it was too early to wake up. Mum did go back to sleep; only this time she never woke up. She was 59.

Health professionals have never been able to confirm whether Alzheimer's was the cause or even a contributing factor of her death. An autopsy was done and the certificate showed a heart attack. Although she'd had similar symptoms to Alzheimer's, they were also symptoms of a number of other mental conditions. Her family and those who knew her before she became ill firmly believe she had a mental breakdown.

She certainly had a lot on her plate, she was teaching English full time at a High School at one point as well as studying for her Open University Degree. On top of this she had me and Ant to bring up - we were around 14 or 15 when her health issues started. Apart from Ant's learning disabilities I had severe asthma and atopic eczema at the time. I'm sure seeing her daughter struggling to breathe and ripping her own skin to pieces on a regular basis would have been horrific to witness and being unable to rid the house of asthma inducing allergens due to the sheer amount of clutter must have been both worrying and frustrating.

Of course there was also the ever increasing mess in the house; it had started to gather in every room on every surface. Each time space was needed to do something, for example eating or homework, Dad's junk would have to be cleared first. Clearing the junk usually resulted in an argument because Dad didn't like his stuff being moved.

My mother was a very house proud woman. She loved all things home. She regularly cooked a Sunday roast for my paternal Grandfather round at our house. She made fruit pies using the fruit Dad had grown in the garden, baked cakes, and made her own yoghurt. She also loved to sew and had a Singer sewing machine on which she'd make clothes for me and matching ones for my Sindy dolls. I spent hours watching her sew and remember being fascinated by the row of ducks she could get her machine to sew after inserting a special black plastic disc and pushing the bar with her knee. She hand knitted jumpers, hats and scarfs for Ant and me. She made intricate ball gowns and trouser suits for my dolls.

I remember her getting very annoyed at Dad every Sunday when my granddad came to dinner as she'd have to remove all his stuff from the living room table before she could put the tablecloth on and lay the table for lunch. She also got frustrated when she had to move his stuff every time she wanted to use the sewing machine or the typewriter for her college assignments.

Mum was a happy, lovely and gentle person who was remembered fondly by all who knew her. She loved children and was willing to offer help to anyone who needed it. She worked hard and loved her home and family. I never really knew her as an adult which was a huge shame. There was a kind of role reversal as she became ill and she became more childlike and needed more help with everyday tasks. I knew she struggled to deal with the amount of junk at the house. I found her diaries in the chaos: I've read her thoughts.

I've never been totally comfortable unless the room I'm in has some order in it. My creative moments can't be released unless I'm relaxed. Clutter to me equals confusion and chaos, both of which generate an instant headache. It's the visual equivalent of a migraine, unbearable! If the kids make a mess I like to have it cleared before they go to bed. I am by no means extreme and my house has an acceptable level of clutter and mess. I have three kids, mess is normal.

When I was a child, however, the house and all its extreme clutter had been normal for me. When I moved into my own tidy, dust free haven and realised it was not the way normal people lived, I realised I could never live that way again. It must have been so difficult going from living in a tidy house to a cluttered one and even worse to see your dream house bought new and gorgeous being gradually transformed in front of your eyes to the state that house eventually became. It must have been devastating to see it happening and not to be able to do anything about it. The gradual pick, pick, pick would have worn anyone down.

I don't remember what stage the house was in around the time Mum started to become ill but I know there were piles of stuff in most rooms. It probably was about a third of what it had become by the time Imelda fell off the ladder.

Had any husband or partner of mine ever started acting like that then he would've gone on a long holiday and there would've been a suspicious lump under the patio a week or so later.

Dad was away with Ant in Spain the day Mum passed away and was due home three days later. I decided it was best they didn't know until they got back. There was absolutely nothing they could've done at the time that I couldn't have done myself. I knew it was difficult to get an early flight from a package holiday and they would've been home anyway a few days later. It wasn't easy speaking to him on the phone that night when he rang from Spain as I had to pretend everything was OK when quite clearly it wasn't. I'd also had to sign papers for the brain autopsy ~ my hand refused to write.

Breaking the news to my immediate family was also hard. I rang them and as soon as I heard a familiar voice on the end of the phone my voice refused to work and I could only manage a squeak. Breaking the news to Dad when he arrived home wasn't easy either. I knew it was going to be difficult and managed to enlist the help of the vicar to help me.

After Mum passed away, Dad's hoarding became worse. For the few years when she'd been in the hospital there had been nobody to keep the junk in check and he hadn't appeared concerned about the mountain overtaking his house. From this point his hoarding became pathological.

# Chapter 19

The hospital asked me to collect Imelda at 2pm, luckily Oggy, being a 4x4, is high off the floor and so ideal for a person with a bad back. Ant and I rushed round to finish up and packed Oggy full of stuff, intending to go to the tip before the hospital.

I checked my *office* ~ the back garden at the mountain ~ where I'd spent most of the previous few weeks sitting on a large ground sheet sorting all manner of everything, and spotted three black bags hidden in the trees. I'd hidden them myself: my well-meaning friends had sorted them for me a few weeks earlier, believing I was getting snowed under. They'd decided to help by filling a few bin bags themselves, but this had made me extremely edgy. I knew everything had to be sorted scrap of paper by scrap of paper. I couldn't have asked them not to sort as they genuinely wanted to help and didn't like to see me sitting on the grass surrounded by piles of stuff struggling by myself.

I'd watched as they'd filled bin bags with "just rubbish"; filling two bags in under two minutes whereas on average it took me about fifteen to sort-and-fill one. They'd told me, "Don't worry, we've checked these bags and really, trust us, there's nothing important, we've checked." I'd sneaked all three behind a tree aside from the fifteen identical looking bags I'd already sorted which were lined up on the path ready to go, intending to double-check the three bags later. I felt dreadful about being so ungrateful to those who had helped but everything had to be checked.

I knew what Imelda was like, his behaviour wasn't normal and I understood it because I grew up with it. I couldn't make sense of it myself let alone explain it to anybody else. And there they were, those three bags, still behind the tree, soaking wet from the night's rain ~ I'd forgotten about them. They couldn't be left for Imelda to find, because if he'd looked through and found something important he would have lost the little, if any, trust he ever had in me.

I had five minutes. I untied the first bag and tried to sort it as fast as I could. There were four-year-old letters. I wouldn't have thrown them out but I could understand why others would. There was a year-old bank statement in an envelope: I took this out ~ oh God ~ there were three whole bags to check ~ at least an hour's work. My hands were shaking now and I had broken into a sweat. A few old envelopes came out, all empty, an old tie, my Mum's old slippers, an empty glasses case, a still wrapped but dust covered pack of tea light candles, some old unused greetings cards without envelopes, then some folded used envelopes. I checked them as I'd checked every other envelope I had ever let go in the bin. As I opened one envelope I caught a glimpse a folded piece of paper with red ink at the bottom – probably some foreign note not visible through the envelope window.

I took it out, my heart started to beat hard and fast and my hands began to shake even more. There were two £50 notes almost mint, folded up in the envelope which had been thrown into the bag. Oh God! That discovery meant each of the three bags would have to be checked thoroughly scrap by scrap. Each of the three bin bags full of "rubbish" would not only have to be smuggled to my house out of Imelda's sight but would also have to go to the tip first and not get mixed up with all the other sixteen ready sorted black bags already in the car. Oggy was stuffed full. She had no boot, so the seats were folded down and there was only just room for Ant to squeeze into the passenger seat. I couldn't hide the bags to come back later as Imelda was coming home and I couldn't risk him finding them and ruining all my past four week's work. I found some string to tie on the bags to identify them and squashed them into the car.

This incident only reinforced my belief that I and I alone, should check every single scrap of paper. I now had doubts about myself ~ had I sorted too casually and too fast? What had I missed?

We finally headed for the hospital via the skip. At the bottom of the road I screamed ~ the three bags for sorting would still be in the car when we collected Imelda from the hospital. Oggy had no boot. The only thing I could do was wedge them behind the back seat and let Imelda sit in the front. There was no alternative.

I had to park quite a way from the hospital entrance and walk over. The plan was to go in and see if Imelda was ready. Ant could then wait with him at the entrance while I fetched the car and drove to the hospital entrance to pick them both up. Imelda had to wear a back brace 24/7 for at least the next three months and it wasn't right to make him walk far. I was rushing and panicking and stressed all at the same time: I had to collect Imelda, take him home and then get to work by 3:30. I was still wearing my stinking, dusty, bogging vest top and my scraggy ripped jeans. I had planned to go home and change first but that wasn't going to be possible!

I rushed through the hospital grounds, through the hospital and on to the ward like a woman on a mission. I'd decided to start with a no nonsense attitude from the word go. People parted in front of me like the Red Sea for Moses ~ they seemed to realise I meant business. I got a lot of strange looks, presumably because I looked and smelled like a bag lady. I got to the ward and Imelda asked what the hell I had on my head. It was only at that point I realised I had just been to the skip and then walked through the whole hospital with a dust mask still perched on the top of my head!

By the time we'd collected Imelda and his belongings, loaded him into the car and taken him home it was quite late and I was cutting it fine to get to work on time. I dropped him home, he thanked me for the lift and I rushed off to work.

At break time later that evening, I rang Imelda at the mountain as I'd been busting a gut to see what he thought of his *tidy* house. I was out of luck because he'd gone to bed for a snooze ~ the first time he had slept in his own bed, without sharing it with piles of papers, in years. I'd also put new sheets on it for him. Ant told me Imelda was quite happy with the "new" house. He also said he'd told Imelda that he thought I'd appreciate some thanks for all my hard work. I was kind of hoping he'd thank me by himself without any encouragement.

At 11pm, Imelda himself rang me at home and said he was impressed with the effort we had made at the mountain although he hadn't had a proper chance to look around yet. He said he'd do this the next day. There followed a silence and then...

'Thank you!' he said... *Breakthrough!*

# Chapter 20

Days after Imelda came out of hospital I was contacted by the editor of a programme about hoarders that was being planned for Channel 5. It was to be a documentary giving a sympathetic angle from the point of view of the hoarder. They stated it was not their intention to make the hoarder look sad and pathetic or a subject for ridicule, but to treat hoarding as a medical condition. I thought taking part would be an excellent plan, because hoarding needed recognition.

It was not my decision though: it wasn't my house or my hoard. I had to run it past Imelda first. I wasn't sure whether he'd be up for it. I'd seen similar shows which managed to ridicule the sufferer even if only indirectly. The advantage, as I saw it, was the possibility of specific and tailored professional help and contacts for the future. I asked Imelda about it and he didn't give me an outright "no", so that was a start. He said he wanted more information and that he'd think about it. This usually meant "No ~ but I can't think of a good enough excuse right now." I didn't hold out much hope.

I went to the mountain at 11:00; I was really eager to hear his feedback. The last time he'd seen the house it was the worst it had ever been. It was now the best it had been in many years. In six weeks I'd removed almost daily car-loads of stuff; ground my knuckles to the bone; given myself a stiff back; gone through six inhalers; missed my kids' summer holidays from school; found a whole stash of money; cleared and refilled two rooms and half his bedroom; changed his bed for the first time in years; uncovered his kitchen table and aged by about two decades. Hell, I was proud of my achievements and I wanted acknowledgement of my efforts at the very least.

Now Imelda was finally home, my efforts would inevitably grind to a halt. If he'd asked me to continue, I would have. However, I very much doubted he'd ask and my own house was seriously in need of some TLC.

I took with me a few boxes of bits from the mountain that I'd taken home to sort. I returned all his books, a set of silver egg cups which I'd polished, a few bits and pieces and all the cash I'd found over the weeks, which amounted to £439 in notes plus a large bag of coins and some foreign currency. I also had some of his pies and fruit from his garden. Imelda had an agreement with some neighbours: he gave them lots of fresh fruit from his garden and they used it to bake pies, one of which they gave back to him. He had six fresh pies stacked up the day he fell, and I'd put them in my freezer for when he came home. I took three round that day.

When I arrived, Imelda was eating breakfast. I gave him the money and told him how much was there. He put the bag on the kitchen table without saying a word. I asked him what he thought.

He looked at me irritably and said, 'Yes, there may well be £439 there!' There was no surprise, no gratitude, no 'Thank goodness you found it,' in fact nothing at all to suggest that such a sum lying forgotten around the house was anything out of the ordinary.

He took the pies from me, saying, 'Oh yes, I wondered what happened to those.' I went upstairs to put the other bits away and he followed me up, surprisingly fast for somebody with a broken back. It was almost as if he didn't trust me to be up there alone.

'Did you find a bed in here?' he asked. This would be an odd question in a normal house, but not in this one.

'Yes,' I said, 'we did.'

'You haven't thrown *that* out have you?'

'Yes, we have Dad. It was forty years old, rotten and it had collapsed in the middle. It was full of moths and it was filling up an unused bedroom.'

He looked disappointed. 'But I was thinking I could sleep on it if I needed to.'

'Dad, I just told you. It was totally rotten, full of moths and dust and had no support ~ it wouldn't have been healthy for you to sleep on it. I spent four whole days just clearing a space around your bed so that you can sleep in there!'

'But there was a spare mattress as well!'

'Yes, and that was rotten too. It was in even worse shape than the first one. It had a huge hole in it, was full of horsehair and when we folded it in half it stayed folded. It was the one I had when I was a kid.' I thought back to my childhood years in that room. Given my allergies to animals it was no wonder I spent most of my childhood fighting for breath and I couldn't remember how many times I'd swamped the bed when I was a toddler! 'It was totally useless, Dad. There'd have been no support for your back at all.'

He looked at me as if I'd just insulted his mother.

'Well, if someone needed to come to look after me they could've slept on it.' Whatever planet he was living on, it certainly wasn't the same one as everyone else. I wouldn't have allowed my worst enemy to sleep on that wildlife reserve of a mattress, and certainly not someone who was there to care for me!

I showed him how much space there now was in the bedroom and he seemed to accept this and went back downstairs to finish his breakfast. I finished putting away the stuff I'd brought over with me and went back into the kitchen. Imelda looked up;

'Did you throw out the old ballcock from the toilet?'

'Yes, Dad ~ it was old and rusty and the ball had a hole in it. It was useless so it went out.'

'We needed that in case we had to measure up for the new one!' Really, there's no pleasing some people! Obviously the next few years would be spent with him badgering me to discover what I'd thrown out.

'The council came to collect those two armchairs,' he said. They'd been outside the patio doors for thirteen years.

'I know, Dad ~ It was me who rang them and then organised the manpower to put them outside the front of the house.' Perhaps he thought the fairies had done it. 'The council will be collecting the old washing machine on Monday too, Dad, because they're separate collection types.' I'd already told him this at least twice over the past two weeks.

He said 'They'll need to come separately for the washing machine as apparently they're different collection types.'

'I know that, Dad. I booked them two weeks ago. I told you that.'

'All right, all right,' he said, 'I'm just *telling* you. Why *won't* you listen?'

At this point I said, 'I'm not staying long today, Dad, I've got loads to do.'

He then asked me to wait as he didn't want to rush his breakfast. I waited, and then waited some more while he poured himself yet another cup of tea. I tried to make conversation and asked if he wanted me to move a box full of tools from the kitchen worktop.

He said, 'I can't hear you with that stupid thing on your face.'

'That stupid thing, Dad, is what I need in order to breathe in this house.' He pretended not to hear.

Finally I got fed up with waiting for him to finish breakfast. I had too much to do at my own house having neglected it so much over the previous few weeks.

'I'm going now, Dad.'

He looked up irritably, 'I thought you wanted me to find you something to do!' he said.

Somehow I managed not to beat him to death with the kettle. I left, fast. I wasn't happy. I was so wound up I had to drag my friend to the pub for lunch and a few beers. Did Imelda really think I had so little to do that I needed him to find me something to keep me occupied? Unbelievable!

As I left, I passed the washing machine outside the house awaiting collection. There was a bare cable sticking out. The lead and plug had been cut off...

# Chapter 21

One thing about searching through a house where nothing has been thrown out in thirty years was that sometimes things were uncovered which you were thrilled to find. Others should have remained buried.

At the very bottom of a box which I had taken home to sort were five sheets of scrap notepaper folded in half. I picked them up to glance at them to see if they were important. Odd childlike writing, single words and phrases were scrawled untidily and willy-nilly all over the paper. Some of the writing looked like mine ~ as if I'd attempted writing with my left hand in the dark after a few too many beers. Weird! I couldn't remember writing it. One of the phrases was "I'm sorry I've been grumpy but I couldn't breathe." I had a strange sensation while I was reading it as if the blood had drained out of my body. I froze ~ I knew what these bits of paper were.

Aged 22 I had a respiratory arrest. This happens when a pair of lungs decide that enough is enough ~ stick this for a game of soldiers ~ and they shut down. When your lungs stop, so does everything else ~ within a very short space of time.

I'd been rushed to the hospital by ambulance about two hours before it happened, suffering from an acute asthma attack, and had been put in a side room to be monitored. I remember feeling utterly terrified. I was alone in a small room and my breathing was deteriorating fast. I couldn't walk or even shout to get help and there was nobody about anywhere.

The nurses finally came to get me for a chest x-ray. I remember one of them saying, quite curtly, 'We don't know how to treat you if we can't see what's wrong.' They wanted me to lie back while they did the x-ray. I couldn't lie back. I needed every inch of lung space I could muster and lying down would reduce it. I was sitting rigid and leaning forward. The nurses got impatient and told me I *had* to lie back. I didn't have the breath to argue. I was absolutely terrified. I took one final breath and ...

Blackness.

I was immediately put on a ventilator, also known as a life support machine, zonked unconscious with drugs so I didn't fight the machine and whisked to the intensive care unit. The machine breathed for me and kept me alive for four days to give my poor lungs a break. I've since been told that at one point it was touch and go whether I'd come back at all. My parents were telephoned at 5am and told to prepare for the worst.

All I remember of that time on the ventilator was having majorly weird dreams. To this day I remain convinced that it was my choice whether or not to come back from the twilight zone. At the time it was no big decision. It was almost as if God was saying, "Hey mate ~ Do you want to die or you want to live? Your choice, let me know when you're ready, OK. Oh, and just tick the box if you want ketchup with your fries, OK. Catch ya later."

I decided I wanted to live; so I did.

Those pieces of paper were my attempt at communication during my time in intensive care. I was connected to the ventilator by a tube down my throat and another up my nose, my arm was strapped up to all sorts of machines and I had wires and tubes almost everywhere. I couldn't talk and I couldn't use my hand properly, so I'd attempted to communicate with people by scrawling abstract words on scraps of paper. I was well away with the fairies at the time because of the drugs, and stayed there for about ten days.

Apparently I'd attempted to apologise to everyone for being grumpy. The nurses told me that the hospital chaplain had come to visit me and had put his hand on my head to bless me (or give me the last rites ~ I can't remember). I had so many wires and stuff everywhere I didn't want to be touched anymore by anybody so when his hand touched my head I threw a wobbly and told him, loudly to "F\*\*\* Off". I've been told that this happens a lot and I'd been forgiven. Perhaps it was excusable with the amount of drugs they had pumped into me.

I'd scribbled a request for an orange Aero bar; odd that was the first thing I'd wanted when my appetite returned. I also asked how my boyfriend was as he'd come to visit, seen me attached to the machine and had fainted splat on the floor, the wimp!

I'd also tried to convey on paper that I desperately wanted to get out of hospital in time to go to the Michael Jackson concert a few days later. I had tickets and was really looking forward to it. I'd had a vivid dream while I was on the ventilator that I was on stage with the man himself. I told the nurses about the dream and what he was wearing during which song. However, when I asked if I'd be out in time, the replies from everyone were, extremely vague, "we'll see", and "maybe" they said. I didn't know that I'd actually "lost" four days while I was on the machine! The concert had been and gone while I was slipping in and out of consciousness and I'd already missed it. Nobody had the heart to tell me this after what I'd been through. Strangely though the outfit I'd described Michael Jackson as wearing during the "*Dirty Diana*" song was actually accurate!

I wasn't sure those memories should have been resurrected, but decided to keep the scraps of paper for the time being. I don't know why.

I was angry with myself that I'd actually apologised for causing so much worry ~ as if I blamed myself for having asthma! I know I was very emotional due to the drugs and perhaps there was an element of relief and gratitude that I was alive which made me apologise.

In retrospect, I doubted anyone had mentioned to the hospital staff that my bed at home was filled with horsehair and the dust in my house was severe to extreme.

# Chapter 22

Shortly after that episode in my life I ditched the wimpy boyfriend and decided I had to get away from the house completely. For a 22 year old my health wasn't good. I was constantly itching, wheezing, sneezing and covered in a rash. Oral steroids for asthma were a regular part of my life and my eczema was so bad my main priorities when looking for jobs were that any uniform wasn't short sleeved and there were no animals.

I was a regular inpatient on the Dermatology Ward and was on first name terms with all the nurses. I spent up to three weeks at a time as an inpatient wrapped in messy zinc bandages and greasy, foul smelling ointments. I had so many skin infections the GP feared I would become penicillin immune. I'd been asked many times to be a prime example of an atopic patient at the University Hospital of Wales training courses, lectures and exams for the Dermatology Professor and his medical students. I had PUVA light treatment which involved standing nude inside a Dalek-like machine full of light tubes for a number of minutes three times every week. I had to wear sunglasses all day during the treatment days because the tablets I had to take made my eyes extra sensitive to sunlight. I had a fair few odd looks and comments walking through the main street in Cardiff in my motorcycle leathers wearing sunglasses on a rainy afternoon in November, I can tell you, "I'll be back," being one of the regulars.

I also had regular visits to the outpatients department at the hospital where doctors told me I had severe asthma and my lungs were similar to those of a fifty year old smoker. Neither I nor any of my family had ever smoked. My lungs had been damaged by the asthma attacks I'd had ever since I was three years old. I also had allergic rhinitis where I was unable to breathe through my nose for years. Whether or not the allergies and atopic conditions were due to the dust in the house was not established but I'm certain they didn't help.

I had to get away from that house while I still had the chance. I'd always wanted to travel and see the world and noticed that every time I'd been on holiday the asthma had been non-existent. I needed to get as far away from the house as possible, but I wasn't able to afford my own place. I believed working abroad was my best option.

I'd already spent a few summers working with PGL holidays in Brecon in Wales as a kids' rep. I'd noticed that my asthma was very much better when I was away from home. Once a week, though, I'd head home for my day off and it would return. Drastic action was necessary.

I'd always loved skiing and felt comfortable and happy in the mountains. I was in love with the fresh air, the mountain scenery and skiing ~ and I could ski hard and fast without the asthma affecting me at all. I didn't even get short of breath and could ski for miles with the best of them without even thinking about my inhaler. I applied for a job with a British company called School Plan which specialised in taking school groups abroad and took over whole hotels for the winter season. They employed British staff and took British school groups to the French Alps. The ski staff, hotel staff, bar staff and reps were all British.

I got a placement in the Front De Neige hotel in Les Carroz. By mid-December that year I was on a ski-coach with other young resort staff heading for France for four months in the mountains.

I tried to keep diaries while I was travelling and working abroad and one of those diaries from my ski seasons was also in the box from Imelda's house. Flicking through, one entry caught my eye: a memory as vivid as the day it happened. The diary entry was actually written on the bus at 03:07 French time on April 16th 1987, on the way home from a ski season in Les Carroz. The resort had closed for the summer; the hotels had all been cleaned and packed up. The staff coach had come to pick us all up and just started the long journey home. After five months of hard work each day in the ski resort, skiing, partying and drinking, most of the staff on the coach had fallen asleep.

I sat at the front as the coach made its way down the dark, twisty, mountain road. I had a thrilling view of the mountain roads from there as I tried to fall asleep.

Watching the road fall away sharply from the verges I was thankful I was on a bus with a professional driver who was used to the roads and glad that I didn't have to drive myself.

I noticed a particularly sharp bend over a cliff that looked a bit hairy, with a giant drop over the edge. I sleepily glanced at the driver. It always amazed me, the way they took such roads in their stride.

The terrifying roads were one thing although the roads paled into insignificance compared to what I saw next; the driver was falling asleep at the wheel!

I frantically poked my mate to wake her, but everyone except me was in a deep sleep. I was living a nightmare. I realised it was up to me to make sure we didn't all end up sleeping forever! I tried chatting to the driver to keep him awake; however the driver didn't speak English and my French left a lot to be desired. I carried on and on talking pidgin French at him, desperate to stop him dropping off in both senses of the word ~ but he kept drifting off to sleep. It was like a horror film.

If I'd gone to wake the others, we'd probably have all been off a cliff before I'd managed it. I just had to keep talking. There were a fair few scary moments and I was exhausted. While I talked and all this was going on, I was logging it in my diary. The crash investigators would be interested in this diary should the unthinkable happen!

Finally daylight came and we stopped for a break at the bottom of the mountains. I was so relieved and told the others who probably thought I'd been imagining things. Oddly, however, in 2013 a coach on the same road at the same time, bringing staff home from a ski resort actually crashed off the mountain road. Fortunately, most of those passengers were unhurt.

When I finally got safely home, I again cleared my bedroom of the clutter that had crept in over the four months I'd been away. As I cleared, the dust flew. By 2am I was wearing an oxygen mask in the back of yet another ambulance on the way to the hospital.

This had become the norm for me; I had to get out. Hell, I had survived the mountain bus only to end up in hospital with asthma. Something had to be done. Winter was eight months away but I needed to get away before that, so I decided to do a season in a summer camp in America.

A few months later I was heading for Kennebec Camp in Maine USA for a summer working as an office assistant. I met some wonderful people while I was there ~ including *the* Mr Michael Douglas, with whom I spoke on the phone a few times when his son Cameron was at the camp.

I loved Maine: it is a really beautiful place teeming with the kind of wildlife we don't see in the UK ~ moose, porcupines and skunks. In summer it was hot enough to swim in the lake. In the evenings we lay on the jetty by the shore of the huge 'Salmon Lake' and watched fireflies playing above us in the moonlight.

It snowed in Maine for most of the winter and there were ski resorts there. The locals strapped snow ploughs to the front of their pick-up trucks and life carried on as normal. The whole town didn't grind to a halt because there was a rumour of a snowflake in the area, as tended to happen in most cities in the UK.

I loved the way the Americans were so straight talking and told it as it was, although I had a few issues translating their sense of humour as they did with mine. I found sarcasm was wholly misunderstood.

After my summer in Maine I decided to travel around America. None of my friends wanted to come so I went by myself. I bought a Greyhound bus pass for ten days and used it to travel from Waterville in Maine to Los Angeles. My first stop was New York. I had no planned route other than to get to Los Angeles in time for a Trek America Tour which left two weeks later.

At the Greyhound Bus station in New York I saw a row of about thirty buses, between them going to almost every place I'd ever heard of. I selected the bus marked 'Dallas'. I was the only white person on the whole bus other than the driver and one of only four women! In a strange place and alone far from home this made me somewhat nervous, so I put my coat over my head and pretended to sleep. At 3am or so there was a huge thud on my shoulder. Fearing a mugging, rape or murder my heart started beating wildly. When I realised that the huge chap in the seat next to me had fallen asleep ~ on my shoulder, I figured it was best not to move or breathe until he woke up. I stayed in that position for what felt like hours. The rest of the journey to L.A. was pretty uneventful and I arrived there ten days later. I slept on the bus most nights, stopping off to visit various landmarks on the way. I visited Graceland's in Memphis and did the Elvis tour which was very exciting. I also did the Dallas television location tour in Dallas and some fantastic shopping in Texas.

To ensure my security while I was alone travelling America, every day without exception, I sent a postcard home, timed and dated at the moment of posting. It stated where I'd been, where I was going, who I'd been with and any other information I could think of.

In theory, when I got home I could put all the cards in a postcard album as a record of my trip. If anything had happened to me at least my last known position would have been documented. God only knows why this made me feel safe, but it did. I was twenty-two and all alone in America and the confidence this gave me was empowering.

As it happened, all my cards reached home, usually in batches ~ two or three on one day and then none for a week. Of course Imelda kept them all, but by the time I got home most of them were lost, buried under the piles of stuff in the house.

Twenty-four years later, I'd been reunited with them, though there were still one or two missing. In the same box I found letters I'd written to Mum and Dad while I was travelling which brought memories flooding back. I had Imelda to thank for those ~ I'd probably have thrown them out years ago.

I finally arrived in Los Angeles after two weeks on the road and was met by a cousin of Imelda's who lived there. I had pumped myself full of oral steroids because she had a Labrador dog. Her house was clean but I was extremely allergic to the dog so ended up sleeping in a tent in her garden for the three nights I was there.

The route back from Los Angeles to New York was on a "Trek America" minibus with nine other like-minded adventurous souls. We met up in Disneyland, California where the only Disney character I met was Tigger ~ the others were apparently all in a meeting that day.

We spent the next three weeks travelling, sightseeing and camping our way back to New York.

From Los Angeles we went to Monument Valley and camped overnight by 'The Mittens', where they filmed the Marlborough cigarette adverts in the 1970s. It was a vast orange desert with two huge rocks shaped like a pair of mittens. The rest of the group took a horse trek around the valley. I couldn't go with them due to the animal allergy so remained at camp. I was totally alone in the desert. It was somewhat surreal. I sat in total silence and watched the sunset.

When the others returned we all sat and chatted round the campfire. I've never seen so many stars in one night. Awesome! Talk about chilling out!

We drove on to Las Vegas where we hired a stretch limo to tour the city; these were still classy back then. We saw all the famous landmarks including the volcano display outside the Mirage hotel, we giggled at the themed wedding chapels and we gambled a few dollars in the casinos. There wasn't a lot to do in the daytime in Las Vegas ~ it's a night time city, but there was a 'Wet 'n' Wild' water park right in the middle where we spent the day.

After Las Vegas we drove on to Zion Canyon National Park, Utah for a day. There were huge orange rocks all blown smooth by the wind. I don't think there's anything similar anywhere on earth.

That evening we drove on to Lake Powell in Arizona. Lake Powell is a similar landscape to the Grand Canyon but full of water. Apparently rain is very rare there although the day we were there it rained hard all day. We did a spot of water skiing on the lake the following day which was exhilarating. I even managed to stay above the water for about 500 metres although with somewhat less style than the others.

When we arrived at the Grand Canyon the following day, we set up camp so we could watch the sunset and sunrise which were amazing. The sound of pan pipes playing as the sun went down will be etched on my memory forever.

The following day, the rest of the group decided to spend all day half killing themselves by hiking right down the Grand Canyon and back up. The tour guides told us

"You'll only ever get the opportunity to do this once". Never a truer word spoken; I didn't fancy my chances of making it down, let alone back up again so I spent the day shopping and bought the *I hiked the canyon* T-shirt instead.

Next we went on to Santa Fe, New Mexico for a spot of shopping and a tour. I went inside the Cathedral of St Francis of Assisi which was the oldest in America. I've always loved old Churches and Cathedrals although unfortunately we had very little time there and had to move on.

We arrived at Carlsbad Caverns later that day just in time to see hundreds of thousands of bats fly out of the cave at dusk. They looked just like black smoke clouds and were all a lot noisier than I'd expected. We went deep into the caves later on which went into the earth the depth of an 82 storey building; thankfully, there was a lift to come back up. They were selling cheap plastic capes outside. I didn't think I'd need one and I slipped on a jumper instead. Big mistake! The capes were to protect the wearer from an onslaught of slimy, slippery and extremely smelly bat poo.

Del Rio, in Texas was our next overnight camping stay. That evening we nipped over the border to Mexico to have dinner. The difference between the two countries was obvious as soon as we went over the bridge. None of the group felt safe walking around Mexico alone so we all stayed closely together.

Following that we went to San Antonio in Texas where we saw the Alamo and walked along the river at dusk. It was a bit like Paris with all the little cafes alongside the river and the lights reflecting in the water.

After we left San Antonio, we stopped the bus and had our lunch by the side of the Rio Grande.

On from there to New Orleans which appeared to be in its own time zone. Nobody appeared to wake up until ten. The shops and cafés opened at about eleven and it was normal to go to bed at three or four in the morning. We went to Bourbon Street, had a swamp tour and ate alligator in a famous restaurant. My postcard said it tasted like chicken.

Next we drove to Ocoee in Tennessee and finally up to Washington DC where we had a whole two days to walk around. We saw the aircraft museum and went up inside the Washington Needle. We saw the White House all lit up at night and the huge statue of Abraham Lincoln.

The following day it was on to New York for the end of trek party which unfortunately I missed as I flew home that night.

All my postcards and attendant memories from back then had been "put somewhere safe" by Imelda and I only found them the day I sorted that box. They had lain in Imelda's house for over twenty years. I took them out and put them all in an album, as I'd always intended. I finally had my album diary of the trip.

While I'd been in America my asthma had been virtually non-existent apart from the relative with the dog in L.A. As soon as I got back to the UK and back to the house it returned with a vengeance. Within four days of my return I was again in the hospital on a nebuliser. Another course of steroids and I was back at the house. I really had nowhere else to go. I had to get out again and fast.

# Chapter 23

I still had the unfinished task of sorting through some stuff from the house after Imelda's return from hospital.

During the weeks following his release I managed to take lots and lots of boxes of stuff back to my own house to sort through. Imelda wouldn't let me throw anything out when he was there but I'd sneak round while he was in the garden, grab a few boxes of stuff and return home with them to sort at my leisure.

In one of these boxes I found several letters which had been written home by me from 1987 to 1992 when I was travelling around the French Alps and North America. They were an insight to my thoughts at the time and brought back some wonderful memories of my travels.

I'd spent five years in total working in French ski resorts Les Carroz, Les Orres, Valloire, Crest Voland and Flaine. I'd also done a winter in a family-run ski resort called Eaton Mountain near Skowhegan in Maine USA.

During my winters away I was able to ski for five hours a day every day for four months each year ~ blissfully asthma free. That was my idea of pure Heaven. I'd become an excellent skier. My health issues never bothered me out in the mountains. I was healthy and as a result a lot more confident. The real me was able to surface while I was away from home. When I was home and struggling to breathe and covered in red raw itchy skin I became shy and lacking in the confidence which I knew I had inside. Winter was my escape.

I hadn't spoken to Imelda over the weekend after he was released from the hospital, thinking he needed time to reflect and to settle back home. It also gave me time to catch up on my own life which I'd totally neglected for the previous few weeks. No doubt Oggy and I would be needed the following week to provide chauffeur services to take him to the doctor, the grocer and the carpet shop among, I suspect, many other places.

He called me at 7:30 one evening. 'Do you remember seeing the charger lead for my shaver?' he asked. 'It was on the top in my bedroom.'

'Er, no, Dad. But as I've said before, I wouldn't have thrown it out.'

'Well where is it then?'

'Dad, I've no idea. I tried to keep everything in the room it was found in. Try one of the twenty boxes in your bedroom.'

'Well, I'll look for it, but you see, in this scenario "if in doubt, throw it out" should not apply.'

Through gritted teeth I pointed out, somewhat curtly, that this had never been my motto and it was more like "if it's not absolute total and utter junk then keep it." There had been more than enough total and utter junk to get rid of and the motto had worked well.

The problem was his "place" for things had been "on the top in his bedroom". This was a four foot wall of junk which, by necessity I'd had to clear and so was no longer there. Once the pile of junk had gone, the shaver plug would have had to go either in a box or in a drawer. As there was still a huge amount of stuff being kept, it could've been anywhere, and, of course, I'd had no one to ask where things should go. It was all down to me.

'Also, do you know where the red vacuum is?' he said.

'The broken one?' I asked. I knew where this was leading.

'Well, it was waiting for parts.' said Imelda. 'You've thrown it out, haven't you?'

'Yes I have.' I said, having already decided I wasn't going to lie about stuff I'd thrown out. I didn't want him to go looking for items which were at the bottom of a council tip.

'Yes, Ant said you'd thrown it out.'

I wanted to enquire why the hell he'd asked if he already knew the answer. Perhaps he was trying to send me on a guilt trip, although that wasn't going to work. It just served to wind me up even more.

'Well until a week ago it was buried under five feet of junk, you hadn't used it for years, and anyway you've got the green one which works.'

'Yes but it was waiting for me to get parts.'

What, for a vacuum cleaner? Getting and fitting new parts would have cost more than a new basic model. I wondered why he needed a vacuum anyway ~ there was only about an inch of floor space in the whole house and judging by the amount of dust in there I didn't think he'd used a vacuum cleaner in years. There had been at least three in the house, only one of which worked and another was still buried under the remaining junk.

'Well, now the house is clearer I want to keep it that way,' he said. 'Besides, we use the vacuums a lot actually ~ to suck up the moths.'

He'd called me to have a go at me for throwing out a broken 23 year old vacuum cleaner. At this point I'd love to say I let it all wash over me but it wound me up something chronic. He'd finally acknowledged the house was now cleaner.

At 8pm he rang again. 'I've found the shaver lead,' he said. Well thank goodness, now I could sleep soundly. 'Have you seen my brushes?'

What! His brushes were two, round, wooden brushes without handles which he used both together, one in each hand, to brush his hairs ~ of which there were very few.

'Dad, I have no idea where your brushes are. Why don't you use one of the 20 or so combs I found instead?'

'Well I like to use the brushes, you see.' He said "you see" a lot ~ it got somewhat wearing.

I began unplugging my phone in the evenings. As Imelda is nocturnal I figured it was my safest bet. He sometimes waited until late to call me, sometimes after eleven. If I'd had a particularly tiring day and night I'd be fast asleep and away with the fairies by then. If I managed to get to the phone, he'd say, "You weren't asleep were you?" Whether I replied "yes" or "no" was immaterial and he'd carry on with his call regardless and of course without apology.

He never called my mobile ~ it was too expensive, though I'd given him my mobile number many times. He didn't own a mobile phone, which wasn't a bad thing in my view. If he'd had one he would probably have lost it or lost the charger.

# Chapter 24

The TV producer contacted me again about the documentary. I still wasn't entirely sure about the idea. She asked if Imelda had made a decision because they needed to start filming soon. She told me that we'd be in a documentary, the first of a series of four looking at OCD and compulsive human behaviour.

The documentaries were each to be themed along the lines of people who couldn't stop themselves hoarding/shopping/collecting/cleaning. No prizes for guessing which one they wanted Imelda for. At this time there were many of these "reality" programmes on television, but the producer assured me this series would be different. It would all be done very sympathetically looking at the situation as a medical issue. They'd look at how the affliction affected the sufferer and their families and how it impacted on their daily lives. This could be used by the medical profession to help diagnosis and future research into the issues and therefore help others. I'd already mentioned the idea to Imelda but made sure I spoke at length to the producer before I asked Imelda for his final decision.

As Imelda had hearing/listening issues I wanted to make sure he was fully aware of everything. Sometimes he didn't catch something that was said and didn't like to ask anyone to repeat themselves. My blog (which the producer had seen) was a bit tongue in cheek and took the mickey a bit. However, the blog was one thing; I knew, more or less, who would be reading it ~ mainly family and friends or others affected by hoarding. However, once the television companies got hold of the story I'd have had no control whatsoever over who saw it. I didn't want my family being ridiculed, insulted or ashamed and was especially wary about Ant being abused or bullied because of his association with it.

I was totally determined that the approach of the programme needed to be sympathetic to the sufferer and not mocking. Many times I'd watched similar shows where the line of questioning left the sufferer open to ridicule and even where background music suggested a kind of comedic feel to the situation. There were also those shows which were popular, let's be honest, in order for the viewer to feel good about themselves ~ programmes with titles like "I live my life on a permanent diet". Inevitably during the programme would be some unflattering footage of said overweight person stuffing a burger and chips into their mouth. Programmes like this only served to humiliate the sufferer. Of course the viewers would snigger behind their TV controls screaming out loud at the TV "No wonder you're a porker!" I had to be certain that they wouldn't do this to Imelda; to be sure they were on the same wavelength as me before I let them anywhere near him. They'd do all their communication and organising through me or it wouldn't happen. They agreed to this.

I wondered how to best approach Imelda about it. Although I'd mentioned it, I wasn't sure if he'd taken the idea seriously or if his comment about thinking about it was just his way of saying no. Finally I just went round and asked him. I explained it would be used to train professionals in the future and could help others to understand the condition which was possibly a medical issue. Imelda said again he wasn't sure; he'd "have to see".

Next day I rang and asked him again, except this time I mentioned that there was a small financial incentive for taking part.

'How much?' he asked, slightly too enthusiastically, and I knew he was more or less sold. He liked the idea of it being on Channel Five ~ he believed none of his mates would be watching. Explaining about catch up TV was not going to help.

The full details were yet to be finalised, but it looked like filming would to start in early October. The producer rang me, very concerned after reading my blog that perhaps I'd done too much tidying before they were able to start filming, and asked how much I'd already tidied. I estimated about fifteen to twenty per cent of the house. Three rooms hadn't been touched at all and one of the rooms was now full again with the stuff that came out of the other rooms. When I told the producer this I am sure I heard her sigh with relief. She asked me to e-mail photos to her as proof though. As she pointed out, different people had different perceptions of what constituted a real hoarder.

As a treat, and because she thought I needed it, my friend had bought me an hour of Reiki. She thought I needed to de-stress. I lay on the couch, mentioned a few pointers to the Reiki practitioner and lay back. I tried so hard to relax. I lay there during the treatment and stared at the pattern on the ceiling tiles and wondered where I could go on holiday. For one whole hour I had to lie still. It was difficult. At the end of the session the practitioner commented on how "wound up" I was and said she thought I found it difficult to relax. However did she know? She gave me some breathing exercises to calm me down. Hmmm, I wasn't entirely convinced breathing would help. I can't say I felt any different when I came out but I didn't feel any worse either and I had relaxed for a whole hour so it had to be good.

On my way home from the school run I nipped in to see Imelda's travel agent who'd been about to finalise his annual jaunt to Benidorm before he fell. Imelda had asked me to tell her about his fall and she'd sent him a card. She said he'd phoned her to thank her for the card and he'd mentioned that he was wondering what I'd done with his gardening trousers as he couldn't find them…

I'd kept the rancid rags, formerly known as his best gardening trousers, and sealed them in a plastic bag. He must have had them at least fifteen years, they were badly snagged, misshapen, ripped, full of holes, covered in paint, stinking dirty and made of some form of navy blue polyester. He had many pairs of trousers, many of which were nice, decent, brand-new and still in their original carrier bags. He'd been wearing these *favourite* trousers when he fell and wasn't in a state to change them. When the A & E doctor came to check him over, his shirt was cut off and I was asked if I wanted to keep the remnants. Hell No! It was one of his tasteless Hawaiian numbers of which he had many. The nurse picked it up between thumb and forefinger with an outstretched arm, as if it were a dead rodent, opened the bin with her foot and dropped it in.

The gardening trousers had now achieved some form of god-like status for surviving not only the hospital but the clear out as well. I knew I hadn't thrown them out ~ not because I didn't think they should have gone out years before, but because I knew he'd have missed them.

I'd explained that I didn't throw anything out except what I knew was rubbish and even then, only things I was pretty sure he wouldn't miss.

Imelda called me a few days later to ask if I knew where his bag of socks was. He'd found a bag of single socks but there was apparently also a bag of clean, paired socks which had gone missing and so he had no socks. I hadn't thrown them out. For someone who had so many pairs of shoes it seemed somewhat amazing he only had one small plastic bag full of socks. I didn't really think it would dent his fine reputation if he were to wear two odd socks. I didn't think anyone would notice.

Tyson desperately needed to go to the dog groomer. Usually Imelda washed the dog himself in the bath and clipped him too. I wanted him done properly before the cameras came and so had called a few dog grooming companies. When I told Imelda the price for a wash and clip was about £50 he was horrified and said he'd wash the dog himself. I had to remind him he had a broken back and so bending over the bath to wash the dog was not one of his most intelligent ideas.

Imelda called me again at 11pm the same day just as I was about to go to bed. He wanted to know if I'd seen his Mrs Beeton's cookery book.

'Do you mean Mum's "dirty book?"' I asked. For years my mother had a cookery book she used to refer to as her "dirty book" because over the years it had been used so much it was covered in cooking ingredients.

'No,' he said, '"Mrs Beeton's Cookery Book". Mum used to call it her "dirty book" because over the years it had become covered in cookery ingredients, so she used to call it her "dirty book" you see.'

'No Dad, I don't know where it is. I know we didn't throw it out, though. What do you need it for at 11 o'clock at night, anyway?'

'We wanted to make scrambled eggs with some eggs we had over.'

'Scrambled Eggs! Dad why the hell do you need a cookery book to cook scrambled eggs for Heaven sake? Even I don't need a cookery book for scrambled eggs and I am renowned locally as being the only woman who can burn water!'

'We needed the measurements,' he said, in a rather matter of fact manner.

# Chapter 25

For once I had the whole day off. I took two kids to school, took the third to the doctor then back to school, went to the chemist for a prescription, posted a letter and got petrol for the car. In the afternoon there was a meeting in the school, then in the evening an open day for the new intake at the local high school for the following year. It had been a fairly quiet day. I liked to keep busy and I was on a de-clutter roll, very likely triggered by dealing with Imelda's house. It was autumn, but I decided a spring clean was the way to go.

I visited Ikea to try to find a solution to Imelda's shoe issue. There were a few cabinets which held up to about ten pairs and even one for eighty pairs but they all needed space to be installed. I gave up on the idea and instead bought myself a flat pack sewing and craft desk. I've always enjoyed assembling flat pack furniture. Call me odd: it wouldn't be the first time.

I looked forward to getting home, putting my music on, making a nice cup of coffee (or beer if I was feeling particularly frivolous) and buying a bag of Galaxy Bites to keep me going. I constructed the whole desk in eighty minutes which wasn't bad even if I did say so myself. I might not have found a solution to the shoe problem, but it had been a great day!

Imelda was getting very excited about the filming the following week for the television programme he'd agreed to take part in. The programme directors had already spoken to him and talked through any of his concerns and I'd also talked him through what might happen and what he had to be careful about saying and not saying. I didn't want them to film the front of the house for fear of repercussions.

I knew the cameras were coming ~ and had an overwhelming urge to go over and tidy up! That, however, would have been defeating the object somewhat.

In my spare moments, I read more of my mother's diaries which she'd written at various times. She seemed to have started writing with all good intentions, carried on for a few weeks, stopped, then picked up a few years later and continued for a few more months. One dated 19.12.1982: "House still in a mess, it gets worse and worse. I get very despondent and feel thoroughly ashamed when I see the playroom ~ especially when he puts the light on. The kitchen is still not finished after twenty years. He says it is getting better but it isn't."

I became determined to find out more about Mum from her neighbours and friends and people who knew her around that time. She wrote about having a long talk with various people. I intended to track down those people. It was so sad that I was pretty much oblivious at the time, being quite young. It was strange that although the mess was evident then, although nowhere near what it was when he fell, in our house, it was normal. I was barely aware it wasn't normal anywhere else.

Mum had told me that Dad had always been an extreme hoarder. So had his mother been, before him. Gradually, despite Mum's best efforts, the floor disappeared under piles of newspapers. I'd become used to sitting on the only bit of the sofa that wasn't covered with piles of newspapers, or on the floor if the sofa was covered completely.

Moving junk from a chair before sitting down to eat had become second nature to me, as was moving three boxes of stuff from in front of the cupboard under the stairs to get my coat every morning for school.

As I grew older I became horribly embarrassed by the mess and rarely invited friends or boyfriends around. I remember Mum's standard phrase when people came to the door; "Please excuse the mess ~ we're decorating".

I even started saying it myself even though it clearly was not the case ~ I felt I should apologise anyway.

I kept my own room tidy and wouldn't put up with anyone else's stuff in it. I spent a lot of time in my room which was the only tidy room in the house. Back then I was a teenager though and this is what teenagers did. I remember feeling that my room was the only room where I had any sense of control and calm. I could relax and read a book. My breathing was slightly better in my room because I kept it dust free ~ although on hindsight, locking myself in a room with a horsehair mattress can't have been wise.

Goodness only knows how I would have handled not having any control of a mess that bad in my own house. Imagine not being able to relax anywhere in your own home because every single room had piles and piles of somebody else's rubbish stacked up. Imagine living with so much rubbish that it was impossible to tidy. There was simply nowhere to put anything anymore. Most people I know needed to have some kind of order in their lives, a place where they had some control. Mum was no different. Everyone needs somewhere where they can relax and be happy. Imagine that your own home was a permanent reminder that you weren't in a happy place and that you had nowhere else to go.

In this situation any normal person would take to going to every friend and neighbour's house they could. There were many of Mum's diary entries to show this is exactly what she did.

I found an interesting entry dated 1984, about the same time she'd started to mention her distress at the mess in the house. "Passed my Open University Degree. Feeling on top of the world."

I returned to the mountain a few days after Imelda came home. The last time I'd seen it, it was relatively tidy. I wasn't daft enough to expect it to stay that way and I'd have been a bit worried if it had. The stairs had been totally clear as this was one of the health assessor's requirements for him to come out of hospital.

When I returned there was a sponge, a brush, a pot of varnish, a coat and a sink plunger on the stairs. To be fair to Imelda, a pine stair hand rail had been fitted by the council. For his own reasons he'd decided to varnish it to match the other side which was dark wood. I wasn't really sure why the sink plunger was there though.

I took back to the mountain with me some more bits and pieces which, for various reasons I'd moved to my house. I took them into the house to put somewhere safe. I went up the stairs to the bedroom and Imelda was there behind me watching me like a hawk. He must have cleared those stairs like a whippet on ice.

'What are you doing? What's that? Where are you putting that? What's that you've got?'

I went into my old bedroom. Most of the stuff in there, which was mine anyway, was taken out by me last month. I moved out in 1994 so there was no excuse for any of my junk to be adding to the clutter. There were a few bits of my stuff from back then in a drawer ~ some scraps of wool and a few unfinished sewing projects. I could see they were all bin fodder but for *my* bin in *my* house. I told him I'd been looking for that stuff and was going to take the bits home. I recognised a familiar trait here ~ my automatic and instinctive reaction of taking rubbish away to put in a bin. I could totally understand now why my mother would have taken stuff to friends, relatives, neighbours, acquaintances, opticians or whoever else had a bin and a sympathetic ear.

I put the stuff ~ my stuff ~ in a carrier bag to take away. Imelda grabbed the bag from me and started sifting through it.

'It's OK it's all mine!' I said.

'Yes, but what is it?' said Imelda, rooting through my stuff.

'It's rubbish Dad ~ from my room.'

'Yes, are you going to throw it out?'

'No Dad ~ I'll take it home to my house for the kids to use.' I'd learned ages ago the truth is not always the best option ~ I lied and I didn't have my fingers crossed so now I will never go to Heaven!

'Oooh, some nice wool here ~ you can use that can't you?' as if I'd probably not actually looked to see what was in the bag.

'Yes Dad ~ the kids will be very pleased with it.' (More lies ~ I'd have to go to church at this rate.)

I pointed out some brand new books I'd found while clearing, they were hard-page, bulletproof books designed for babies of about a year to eighteen months old. A baby could chew the books, get sticky fingers all over them, hit the cat with them and possibly puke on them. No baby would ever be able to actually read the books but the parent was supposed to do that while the baby looked at the pretty pictures. They were lovely Winnie the Pooh books; two sets of three books. When I asked him about them he said he'd got them for my kids but had "mislaid them temporarily". In other words they'd become buried in the layer of junk corresponding to the year 2003. I asked if he wanted me to take them away to a charity shop.

He said, 'Well, the kids can still look at them can't they?'

I pointed out that my kids were by then reading very well and the books they read no longer had pictures.

As usual he ignored me. 'Yes, well. Perhaps they can have them for Christmas or something ~ I'll keep them for now.' He put them on top of a pile...

I fully expected the books to turn up at Christmas the following year, providing he hadn't lost them again. They'd be wrapped in some obviously "recycled" paper, probably with, "To Granbab, Hape Berfdey" written on it and sealed with masking tape. That was if they were lucky enough to have real wrapping paper: often it was just a carrier bag. Perhaps the books would turn up with the recently rediscovered two left flamenco shoes, one size 5 and the other a size 6. If they were even luckier they might even get a tea towel, as I did for my 21st Birthday. For the record it had 21 pigs on it, one black and twenty pink so he had actually thought about it a bit.

I went outside into the garden where there were still boxes I'd put there the day he came out of hospital, they were damp. I started to go through the pile and noticed Imelda watching me like an expectant pigeon. I showed him three pairs of new wellies I'd found. I realised one was a ladies size 5: my mother's wellies. I said I'd take them home.

'Yes but we don't just throw things out do we?'

He really, truly had no idea at all how hard I'd worked checking and sorting his stuff. He still thought I'd thrown out huge piles of new stuff. I had told him so many times that I hadn't thrown anything out which I thought he'd miss or anything which someone else might have found useful, nor did I throw anything out which he could have reasonably needed to keep. I didn't need to ~ there was enough total and utter rubbish in there which was taking up space.

I'd thrown out piles and piles of old newspapers, but kept some from 1878 which were of historical interest. I'd flicked through every magazine before I threw it out in case there was something hidden inside. I opened every apparently empty envelope. I unravelled every discarded receipt and found £20 notes wrapped in a few of them. I sorted everything with his signature on it and burned those separately. I kept all letters from the previous five years in case he needed them.

I searched through every single item that was thrown out, from old ear buds to old record players ~ including the one which had the accident with my foot. He did notice the record player was missing, but wasn't angry: he wouldn't have dared to be. He did however try the old guilt trip routine many times; today it was his old gardening jumper.

'It was knitted for me by your mother you know. It had a run on the one arm but it could've been sewn up. It was very warm in winter in the garden.' That particular guilt trip wasn't going to work with me. If my Mum knitted it, I was sure she wouldn't have minded me chucking it, under the circumstances.

Later that evening, I finished work and as I jumped into the car a wall of musty air hit me. I'd forgotten about the bag of stuff from his house, which I'd put in there earlier. It had been a warm day and the smell almost knocked me out. Poor Oggy stank of musty feet for weeks.

The following morning I took Imelda some more of his fruit pies from my freezer and a few bits and pieces I'd sorted which were cluttering up my garage. I carried the bits up to my old bedroom which was 90% clear the week before he came out of hospital. It now contained a vacuum cleaner, some suitcases, lots of fluorescent light tubes, an old iron bed frame which wouldn't fit in the car, some picnic hampers and an ice box, two suitcases and a box of files. Also of course there was the faithful old carpet that had been bought in 1977 that had lain, rolled, up the stairs for thirty-six years. When we picked it up and folded it to go into the room, it had cracked and exploded into a cloud of rubber dust ~ the rubber backing having virtually solidified. Imelda was now thinking of putting it down as carpeting in Ant's bedroom. Oh for goodness sake! Not only was it now threadbare in places and moth eaten, the thing had flowers all over it and a design which was made, and in my opinion should have stayed, back in the seventies. It was now a health hazard as well.

I noticed a flat packed furniture box, a small wooden chest of drawers that hadn't been there when we'd cleared the bedroom. I asked Imelda where it had come from. He told me it had been in the garage. As I genuinely enjoyed assembling these flat-pack furniture items and like the wonderful helpful daughter I was (ahem), I offered to do this for him. I wanted to show him I could actually do something just as well as he could, in fact, probably better, since I'd done many of these recently and quite regularly. After a year studying carpentry and wood trades in college I also had a BTEC carpentry qualification with a distinction pass.

I took all the bits out to the garden where the air was fresher. I asked Imelda if he had a hammer because I saw there were pieces of dowel and plastic drawer runners which had to be gently tapped in.

Imelda said 'You don't hit screws with a hammer!' I let this go. One might've assumed that, as he was my father, he would have realised I had slightly more common sense than that. But then, he rarely listened to a word I said and he assumed as I was his *daughter* and therefore *female,* that I was naturally clueless about everything.

He was hovering annoyingly, so I told him to go and take the dog for a walk. He went. By the time he returned fifteen minutes later I'd assembled the main carcass of the chest of drawers and three of the six drawers. The drawers were very tight and the thing did not go together as easily as it should. I asked him how long he'd had the pack in the garage and was told it was about seven years.

He'd kept this wooden flat pack drawer unit for seven years (translates to about fifteen years in real time) in the garage. The thing had warped itself into an interesting shape. I was, however, determined I would get it together. I did this and completed it within forty-five minutes, although the drawers were still very tight. I was hoping it would warp itself back into shape once it had been in the house in the warm awhile.

The stairs had started to accumulate junk again. All the white plastic pipes, conduit and trim which I'd put in the garden during the clear out had been put on the stairs; as they were plastic there'd been no urgency to bring them back in. They could easily have gone in my old bedroom but Imelda evidently preferred to put them on the stairs. I refused to tidy anything away from that point on as the television cameras would be filming the following week and they needed to see it as it was, warts and all.

It didn't take him long to start messing the place up again after he came home. I had to tell myself I didn't care anymore. If he wanted to live in a pigsty then that was his choice. I planned to sneak in at a later date, after the filming, when I knew he was out and clear out some more stuff. I'd sneak in, fill up my Ikea bags, load up Oggy and sneak home before he even had time to realise I'd been in. I'd found lots of interesting stuff in there belonging to my mother, besides her diaries, but I believed there was more to find.

I had a vested interest in the house. Keeping all that weight in an upstairs room wasn't only a strain on the floor but it was a health hazard and more importantly a fire hazard.

One day when he climbs the great ladder in the sky and doesn't descend again; it will almost certainly be down to me to clear the house. I therefore thought I'd save myself stress and time then and start sooner rather than later. It would also be nicer for him to live there meanwhile with less stuff.

The part which I intended to start on was my mother's side of the main bedroom which had been under a pile of junk since she went into the mental hospital in about 1988.

~

The following day was my birthday. I was forty-something and had been summoned to Imelda's house as

155

he needed milk and dog food which was difficult for him to carry.

When I got there Imelda was quick to tell me he'd tightened the screws in the flat pack chest of drawers I'd assembled for him a few days before. He'd done it because he thought it may have made the drawers easier to open. I told him I'd tightened them as much as they would go, mindful that over-tightening a wood screw would simply make the joint loose. The chest of drawers, after its years in the garage was as warped as an 'S' bend. Nobody could've put that chest together so that it opened properly. I asked him if his efforts had made the drawers open any better. He admitted they hadn't. I think he was telling me because he wanted me to know he'd had to go and do the job properly. Clearly I was totally incapable although the drawers still had to be opened with a crowbar and shut with a size ten boot.

Ant had bought me a birthday present, wrapped it in new paper and attached a lovely card. He knew what I liked and the card and gift were lovely. The card had a chimp on the front and said, "As you get older even simple things become confusing..." The card was printed so it opened the wrong way so, like a fool I tried to open it the usual way and couldn't ~ much to his delight.

Imelda said 'I might be able to find you a little something!' I wasn't sure whether I was supposed to be dribbling in anticipation at that point. After about twenty minutes of faffing about I said I was leaving as I had to go to work.

I was still waiting in the car ten minutes later. Imelda was never in a rush, unlike me. Eventually he appeared with a Toblerone bar behind his back the way one might hide a gift for a small child. How did I know it was a Toblerone? It wasn't wrapped.

'I haven't managed to find any paper,' he said, and as an afterthought, 'You can eat nuts can't you?' I haven't been able to eat nuts for the past twenty years but that was just a technicality.

'Er no Dad, I can't eat nuts. Don't worry though I am sure the kids will eat it for me.' This cheered him up somewhat and he gave me the Toblerone.

'Happy Birthday,' he said.

The Toblerone was *in date*! He'd bought it recently ~ just for me. Overlooking the fact that he didn't remember I'm allergic to nuts, it meant he actually went to a shop and bought it for me! I did feel slightly special. He also gave me a birthday card in which he had thanked me for my help over the past few weeks.

The bloke and the family took me out for lunch to my favourite restaurant in Cardiff Bay. They put helium filled balloons on the table for me and we took them home. The kids made me take them to work so that I'd feel happy. I took them in and the team wished me Happy Birthday.

After break we were told we were having an emergency team meeting. Heck! We all gathered round and they'd bought me a load of cupcakes, a card, and some chocolate. I was touched.

# Chapter 26

Because nothing was thrown out, clothes I threw in the bin years ago in my teens, were turning up. Most of these things should've stayed thrown out when I discarded them in the seventies, especially some of my more dubious fashion disasters. I was a bit of a one in a fashion sense back then; lots of black, Goth and Punk stuff. The clothes re-surfaced recently and to make sure they were finally gone, I threw them in the skip myself.

Another problem was the smell. Nothing had been washed for years and it all smelled horrible, the same smell that penetrated throughout the house, a mix of sweat, dust, musty mould, wet dog, old person and feet. One or two of my shirts and jeans from back then also re-surfaced and they were, ironically, back in fashion. They were too big if anything as I appear to have become skinnier, although I remember in those days, anything big and baggy was the thing to wear. Sadly though, the clothes ponged something chronic. I tried washing the clothes on a very hot wash and only just managed, after the third wash to get rid of the smell. It was like having a whole new wardrobe all for free.

I remember going to London on the bus with a mate wearing a micro mini skirt with blue and black striped tights, about six chain belts, black fingerless lace gloves with black nail polish, a Carnaby Street jacket with pins, zips, chains and studs and a black geisha style wig with an electric blue fringe and a matching blue bow. To match this we had blue lipstick and thick black eyeliner. I thought I was the bat's danglies at the time. I found a few of the belts and the wig last week. I had to have those back, purely for fancy dress purposes you understand.

I remembered, back then, every time I put something in the bin it would resurface in the house weeks or months later. Perhaps I could have been a bit sneakier and liaised with the neighbours to use spare space in their bins. For a time I thought I was going loopy. Things I knew I'd put in the bin kept reappearing like some insane Groundhog Day. I remember confronting Imelda a few times only to be snapped at: he hadn't sorted through it yet or it could be burned as fuel on the open fire. I'd put stuff in my bin in my room. He'd empty the bins, like most houses in the UK I guess. But unlike most houses, he'd then sort through everything and bring back in anything he wanted to keep.

Back then there was no sorting and recycling. Rubbish was rubbish to be put out in a black bag for collection. Why then did he feel it necessary to sort through everything?

Perhaps a hoarder thinks differently from regular folk. A "normal" person might think, "Aha! I've had this jumper for three years, I've not worn it very much, it wasn't one of my better fashion decisions, it also has a hole in the front and is has become very tatty and stretched. It's no good for charity so therefore I'll put it in the bin".

A hoarder, however, thinks, "Aha! A jumper that I've only had three years! I see it has a hole but this can be sewn up; I see it is stretched but it is still wearable. Perhaps I'll keep it to wear around the house. I see the design was a bad decision but hey it may come back into fashion, besides, nobody will notice ~ I'll keep it to one side just in case". That "one side" over time becomes a dusty pile which has more and more and more "just in case" items piled on top of it until it is buried and forgotten. Months turn into years, possibly decades. Finally it becomes just one enormous pile of rotting "just in case" things which all merge into each other. Individual items become a wall which in turn becomes part of the landscape in a house whose interior is strangely shrinking at the same rate that the "just in case" items are being kept. Eventually all the hoarded items are forgotten and none can be found in the rare event they're even remembered.

I found a whole stack of Cosmopolitan magazines from 1989. These were very funny as the fashion and the articles were now so very dated. One article was 'Our lives in 2020'. The magazine editors had tried to predict what life would be like in the future. Some bits such as the mobile phones were spot-on but others were way off the mark.

In the same box was a letter I had written on 3rd April 1989 when I'd been working in Les Carroz ski resort in France in a hotel called *Le Front de Neige*. After four months of being away for the whole winter season I'd just been given the date for my return to the UK and was writing to let them all know at home. My final paragraph of an eight page letter said, in capital letters;

"WHEN I GET HOME I WOULD LIKE MY ROOM INTACT, FREE OF RUBBISH, JUNK AND DUST, AS I LEFT IT, READY FOR ME TO MOVE BACK IN". It was clear that I almost expected Imelda to have filled it with junk, odd bits and rubbish. From memory, he did not disappoint.

That was yet another year I was ambulanced to hospital with an asthma attack the same day I got home from a season skiing in the mountains.

~

Today the cameras were due to arrive to start filming. Imelda was quite excited. The camera crew were due at base camp at noon. I'd spoken many times to the producers in the run-up to filming date and had the impression that they were still a bit concerned that the place would be spotless because I'd spent so long tidying. Oh how wrong they were!

Their fears were soon allayed when they arrived at base camp. They spent some time chatting, getting to know us and looking around the mountain.

Imelda, bless his cottons, had done more tidying up in one day than he had in the past twenty years. The stuff he'd put on the stairs last week had magically disappeared and even the vacuum cleaner was out as if he'd even considered using it! The kitchen table was clear and Imelda had put a towel over the pile of junk in the bedroom as if to disguise it. Bless!

The film crew of two, Imelda, Ant and I all sat at the kitchen table for a cup of tea and a chat. They were both very polite and diplomatic. They'd brought full-body dust suits and high grade filter dust masks, but were quite relieved that they wouldn't need them. They promised to try their hardest to show us in the best possible light and they didn't intend to make us look stupid. They repeated that the documentary was aimed at showing how hard life was from the hoarder and their family's points of view. I told them what they could film and what they couldn't, and why, and they promised to respect this.

We were happy for them to ask anything about the hoarding and both promised to be honest and open. If this was going to work we'd all have to trust each other.

They explained the programme would be about an hour long. Two other people would be featured: a man who'd moved from a large house into a small flat and now had no room for all his stuff and an elderly lady who had become trapped in a downward spiral. Her house was strewn with rubbish, used food boxes and far worse.

They decided to film Imelda sitting in his office: he sat, looking quite pleased with himself. They began by asking when he started hoarding, why he thought he hoarded and what was the last thing he threw out and when.

The big problem was that Imelda has hearing issues. Although he knew the programme would be about hoarding, he seemed to think people would be far more interested in his life history. When asked specific questions he didn't answer them, but waffled on and on about his hobby ~ DIY, and his other hobby ~ more DIY, and his other favourite subject ~ himself. I don't think he heard many of the questions, but instead of asking for a question to be repeated, he burbled on, answering what he thought the question might ~ or should have been. His answers therefore bore little if any resemblance to the question. I think they were looking for about twenty minutes of footage which would be edited to about ten: Imelda chatted for eighty-two minutes. They'd have their work cut out editing that one!

The film crew left for their hotel, planning to return the following day to film a bit more and to ask me some questions for the point of view of a relative. They wanted me to get stuck in at base camp and re-enact those days I spent there all summer.

By the next day the crew had spoken to their HQ and they wanted even more footage. Imelda had impressed them so much with his "crazy eccentric old man" act that they were considering making his story the main theme of the documentary rather than one of the back stories.

That morning, luckily, the cameraman was able to be honest with me. He said he wasn't sure how to tell me, but while Imelda was coming across as a lovely old gentleman with whom the audience were sure to fall in love, all my frustrations with the situation were coming out and I was coming across as quite aggressive. He said that TV audiences could be judgemental and perhaps I'd take that on board for the day's filming. I was very grateful for his honesty.

I'd made the effort to look a bit gorgeous but had failed miserably. I'd heard that television cameras can make a person resemble an albino snowman on a foggy day so in an attempt to look human I'd recovered the slap from the back of the drawer. Sadly my attempts at looking gorgeous made me look like a tipsy drag queen.

They wanted some footage of me as "clearer-upper" and also wanted to interview me. I was OK with that but they wanted to film me in my very unflattering white dust-suit and dust mask. I agreed: it might provide a level of disguise.

When it was my turn to be interviewed, I was a bit nervous having a camera so close and didn't know what to do with my hands but eventually I got used to it.

I'd asked what questions they'd be asking me, but they refused to tell me in case I sounded rehearsed. I was told not to look directly at the camera but at the cameraman, although talking to someone without having eye contact was difficult.

Their first few questions I'd anticipated, so that helped me feel comfortable with the cameras. Then I was asked, "What happened to the record player?" The producer had done his research by reading my blog.

'Um ~ it had an accident ~ with my foot,' I said, realising Imelda wouldn't be pleased with this revelation. I'd have to live with it. I'd put it all on my blog but was fairly confident Imelda wouldn't ever read anything on a computer ~ he doesn't own one. Television, however, was a different matter.

They also filmed Ant, though I was unsure whether he should be in the documentary as I was worried he may suffer repercussions. Because of his learning issues, he tends to get some abuse from certain unsavoury elements of the community and I didn't want to make this worse.

Before they started filming, I'd had to sign lots of forms and have a long discussion with the television welfare department. I was asked if anyone who might appear in the programme had ever had any mental issues or depression. I mentioned my concerns over Ant and they said it would be best not to include him. I asked Ant what he thought, and he said he really didn't mind if he was on it or not. However, when filming began on day two, Ant became withdrawn. I tried to find out why, but couldn't get to the root of it. He kept saying nothing was wrong. I asked him if he wanted to be on the programme. He said he didn't and he went to work.

Imelda asked why I'd said Ant couldn't take part in the programme. He said Ant was extremely upset at being excluded because he felt he wasn't being treated as part of the family. I'd always found this difficult, not only with Ant but with people in general. I've always preferred to be told straight. I can't handle people who say one thing and mean entirely the opposite. I don't have time to study mind reading. Please, just say what you mean and we can move on.

The producer had the final word anyway and it wasn't my decision, no matter what Imelda and Ant thought.

Ant had been at work for most of the time I'd spent at the mountain. The days he was at home he was reluctant to help me get rid of stuff in case he threw something important out and got shouted at by Imelda. Ant, at 47, was still thoroughly intimidated by him. He was totally unable to take the initiative with what to throw out. He'd helped a lot in the evenings by looking inside boxes full of papers and apparently empty envelopes and by helping bring the overnight stuff back inside after I'd finished for the day.

While I was being interviewed, Imelda was rustling about loudly, apparently unaware that they were filming and he needed to be quiet. They stopped filming for a minute to let Imelda walk past and we all turned to see what he was up to. For the first time in thirty years, apparently something had motivated him throw something out! He was caught carrying a huge bag of rubbish downstairs. I'm not sure if he'd engineered the scene and taken the bag upstairs beforehand but it looked hopeful. I didn't think it would last though.

With Imelda about it was impossible to clear up, although I managed to smuggle a few bags out to Oggy while he was tied up with the film crew. I was also keen to recover my Ikea bags from the house before they were absorbed into the mess and became part of the mountain

Imelda saw me taking them out of the house. 'What's that you've acquired?' he asked, as if I was stealing them.

'They're *my* bags, Dad, and I bought them with *my* money. I brought them here and now I'm taking them home.' He wasn't convinced. He's never been to Ikea so I don't know how he thought he'd acquired them.

I was taking out a pile of papers and rubbish but he interrupted me and started looking through them. I abandoned the idea, took it all back in again and hoped he'd forget about them. I could get them another time.

I also found some disgusting rags while they were filming and picked them up between forefinger and thumb as one might pick up a dead mouse. Vile! They looked as if they'd been used to clean up an explosion in a psychedelic vomit factory. At least *they* could go in the bin. I was just slipping them into a bin bag when Imelda appeared. 'Ah! You've found my curtains!'

You couldn't make it up! I'd never seen anything quite so repulsive in my life. Why anyone would want to give them houseroom, let alone hang them as curtains was anyone's guess. Perhaps it's an age thing. If ever I decide something like that is a good idea in my house, please shoot me.

After a few more questions and a lot more filming the crew were happy and left for the day. I was aware that I'd possibly given away more than I would have had I been able to consider my answers first; the record player incident for example. I hoped it would be edited out, because Imelda wouldn't be pleased. He won't read about it here because he doesn't read books.

When the cameras left I rushed home, had a quick wash and went to work. Any hopes of a quiet night were dashed: the run up to Christmas had started and the phones were very busy. There might also have been a full moon judging by some of the calls I had.

# Chapter 27

I went to see Imelda, picking up some shopping he'd asked for on the way. I had a few more sorted bits to return to his house and I was also interested to see what he'd do if I suggested sorting out some more stuff.

I took some of the old "keep" books that I'd sorted at home back into his study and Imelda followed me in.

An unfortunate effect of his hoarding was, if someone entered a room and was followed in, there was no escape unless the second person left first. Imelda had followed me in and I was backed into a corner. He doesn't have much idea of personal space and if he can't hear someone he tends to stick his ear almost in their face which is uncomfortable: I was bending backwards until my back was almost in two.

He shouted; 'Good heavens above ~ what's that beastie there?' Thinking he meant a spider or something I looked where he pointed. Bold as you like, a huge old fox trotted up the front path and past the window into the back garden. It was the middle of the morning and the fox was acting like he owned the place. It gave me an excuse to get out although when I got to the garden the fox had gone.

Next, as planned, I suggested a tidy up. He'd said in front of the cameras, that he'd be grateful if I could help him sort out some of the paperwork.

'I've got a free hour, Dad, so why don't we start now?' I said. Imelda agreed, though I detected a certain air of reluctance.

I went upstairs and he followed, we sat on the bed and I took one of the many full boxes from the pile in his bedroom and put it on my lap. Inside was, in my opinion, pure junk.

The first item in the box was a smaller box, inside this was a third, smashed plastic box. I asked him what it was.

'Oh that's an old meter box from the church; some vandals broke in and smashed it so we had to replace it.'

'OK. So it's broken and has already been replaced so we can throw it out!'

'Well doubtless it *can* go out *sometime.* I just want to have a look through it first.'

'Look, Dad it's smashed, no use to anyone and taking up space, so it can go out. Yes?'

'Well, yes, after I've had a look at it.'

'Here it is Dad.' I handed him the box. 'Have a look at it. Can it go out?'

'Well yes, doubtless it *can* go out when I've checked it.'

'Dad, what is there to check? You've just seen it! It's broken and can't be used ~ Why do you want to keep it?'

'It may be useful for parts.' I gave up on that item at that point. It was from a break-in at the church eight years ago.

Next there was an old paintbrush that had obviously been used, and then cleaned in some form of sticky stuff. It was stiff and greasy with a thick layer of dust. Obviously, here *was* an item which could go out.

'Yuck Dad! A greasy old paintbrush ~ I'll put that in the bin bag.'

Imelda took it from me and put it on top of another box. 'It can be cleaned!'

Next there was an empty used bank coin bag. I put this in the bin bag.

'What's that?' asked Imelda. 'I can use that!'

Next was a five page Christingle order of service leaflet from St Mark's, dated December 21st 2002. Imelda took it from me and placed it on the bed.

'Dad, we aren't getting anywhere here are we?'

'Yes, well, I appreciate your help but I need to sort through these.'

'But that's what we're doing!'

'Yes, I appreciate your help and you can certainly throw some stuff out ~ once I've sorted through it.'

Apparently he thinks *he's* doing *me* a favour by *allowing* me to throw stuff out, that he's already sorted. Gosh, how incredibly thoughtful he is!

I continued taking things out of the box ~ a scrunched up old, used tissue.

'Yes that can go.' Imelda was incredibly pleased with himself for deciding to chuck something! He put it on the bed beside him, not in the bin bag I was holding which was still empty.

Next out was a child's flowery tie, one of Ant's from when he was little in the 1970's and used to wear ties to parties. The tie was faded, shapeless, dusty, musty and the stitching was coming undone. I put it in the bag.

'What's that?'

'Ant's old tie ~ it's BOGGING Dad.'

'Well *someone* may find a use for it.'

Finally I tried the seventh item - an old AA size battery. I put it in the bin and told him I could recycle it when I got home.

'How do you know it's dead?'

'I don't; but since it's been here around fifteen years it's very likely.'

'Exactly' he said.

I put the battery in my pocket.

'You want to keep that do you?' he said, after a few moments thought. I didn't want to keep it, nor did I want him to act like he'd given me a gift. At this point I gave up.

*Mental note to self: return while he's out and just take boxes.* It was impossible to try to sort while he was there.

# Chapter 28

I couldn't carry out my plan that Sunday ~ Cardiff half marathon was taking place and I was a volunteer at the first aid station at the eleven mile point, a lovely spot right next to Roath Park Lake. For the first hour it was quiet: the first runners went through, all athletic looking, serious and focused. Others followed all very fit and healthy looking and I started to think perhaps it would be a quiet day.

Then someone said a runner had passed out some metres back and within about five minutes we had a bit of a busy spot. About seven runners hit the deck simultaneously and had to be scraped back up. They were all taken off to be checked over. The poor souls had no idea where they were and had come over all strange.

If I'd attempted to run thirteen miles I think I'd have come over all strange after about twenty metres. This was why I was at the first aid post and not running the marathon. The ones who completed it had run thirteen miles further than I could've run.

~

The television people contacted us again. They'd showed the original footage to their bosses who also thought Imelda was a bit of a character. They asked if he might possibly agree to them sending round some professional, trained de-clutterers to help make his home liveable.

Once his house was tidy, they reasoned, he would then be able to have his grand-children visit him *inside* his house for the first time ever. There would be space to sit and perhaps watch a film, read a book or whatever with Granddad. This would be filmed and would make a wonderful ending to the documentary. There was also the point that Imelda flapping about would make interesting viewing.

From my point of view, my children visiting Imelda would mean a lot as he's their final remaining grandparent. I think it's a great idea for kids to keep in touch with the older generation, although I'm not sure he's the best ambassador for his age group. He has a lovely big garden where I used to play when I was small and which would've been wonderful for my children to play in as well. There are trees to climb, lots of places to make dens and get muddy, places to hide and explore.

I'd never left them with him for even a short time because it never felt right. When they were young I always preferred to take them with me to the doctor or hairdresser, feeling they'd be safer with me. I was always worried when they were small that in Imelda's house they'd pull something over on themselves or find something dangerous to play with.

There was never enough space for them all to fit into one room at their granddad's house, so they could only visit him if the sun was shining and they could play in the garden ~ and when I was there to haul them away when it was time to go. If the house was clear, though, they could play outside then go inside to watch television or whatever.

I didn't know what sort of training these professional de-clutters had ~ after all each hoarder is as individual as their hoard. I'd read a lot on hoarding over the years: some hoarders' houses were just too full and some had rotting food and often rodents. Sometimes a broken pipe or leaking roof had soaked the inside of a house, which would cause mould and consequent health issues. The hoarder was often too embarrassed to let anyone inside the house to fix the problem and so just ignored it.

I know junk when I see it as I suspect do most people, but Imelda's idea of "junk" differs from *my* idea ~ or anyone else's ideas of junk!

I think a single shoe, so old the sole has disintegrated, is junk. Imelda thinks "keep it ~ the leather strap may be useful for something".

I think an old washing machine, abandoned under a tarpaulin in the garden since 2002, is junk. Imelda thinks "we can keep the plug, and perhaps the drum, and possibly parts from inside".

To me a piece of foam about a foot square with disintegrating edges and sporting a footprint that stayed imprinted in the foam weeks after I pulled it from the bottom of a pile is only good for the bin. Imelda wants to keep it as it is apparently, 'a nice piece of foam'.

On a pile in the living room was the large box of Thornton's chocolates that I'd bought a few years before for his birthday, thinking he could enjoy them while sitting down with his feet up and a nice cup of tea. My first and only thought with these now was 'bin' as not only were they dated best before the end of last year but they'd been lying on top of the mountain of junk in the sun in the front room, where three days ago, while Imelda was out, the dog found them and helped himself. He'd probably been eyeing them up for months. When Imelda got home the chocolates had been half-eaten and scattered, all no doubt well licked. Did he throw the remainder out? No; brown and squidgy as they were, he ate some of them! I suggested this was possibly not one of his better ideas and went to put the remainder in the bin. Imelda replied that the box said "best before" not "eat by" and this just meant they were not at their best after this date. He put them to one side for later.

I mentioned to Imelda that the television company had offered to clear his house and I left him to mull it over. I promised to make sure they wouldn't touch his "office" as this was his very own organised chaos. I told him they'd have to play by our rules if they wanted more footage.

The producers suggested the lounge would be the best place to start ~ the sofa was in there, somewhere, and when it was uncovered it would be ideal for the grandchildren to sit on when they came to visit.

Before the original filming began, in a twenty foot lounge there was one armchair and a little path leading to it surrounded by mountains of stuff. Only one person could watch the television at a time which was very unsociable. If I ever had to go in there, my axe-murderess tendencies rose to the surface. I suffered from almost uncontrollable urges to say, 'What do you want this for ~ can I throw it out?'

Imelda thought it was a huge ask from the television company to want to come and clear out a whole room. He didn't see it as a favour. It was a big job, although it was they who were offering to do all the work. They promised if he didn't want to throw anything out they wouldn't and if he really wanted them to they would put it all back in again afterwards.

On the positive side for Imelda he'd get a chance to look through his things, possibly rediscover hidden treasures, have an opportunity to throw things out and all without lifting a finger ~ or paying a bean. Once the stuff was out he'd have his room back and be able to at least dust and hoover up the moths. He could also organise the stuff coming back in in a more orderly manner, so in theory it would leave him with more room. It might even give him the kick he needed to start clearing. Pigs might fly!

It would also of course help me, because I still couldn't go in the house without full dust protection and even then I struggled to breathe. Their help would be beneficial all round, and would also make his house a much nicer place to live and to visit. He might even be able to have the neighbours round for a drink at Christmas again! All I could see were positives, though I recognised that it might be a very stressful time for him:

he panicked if he saw me taking a bag of my own stuff away, even my unearthed childhood possessions. They wouldn't be allowed to throw anything away without his OK. I'd be there to oversee it as well.

Worst case scenario was that they took everything out, he refused to part with anything and they had to put it all back, but if this happened at least it could be replaced tidily, so there would be more space because it wouldn't just be placed precariously on top of a million other bits of stuff.

I'd given Imelda four days to mull over the professional help idea. I told him whatever his decision it was OK with me. I wanted it to be *his* choice.

Imelda thought the best option was to have a marquee in his garden for a week or so, so he could go through his stuff himself. Realistically this was never going to happen – he would never get round to it by himself. The television company would not allow it as their insurance wouldn't cover it. They also wanted it done in a couple of days as their time was limited.

It was interesting that of my mates I'd mentioned the professional clear out to, half thought it was a marvellous idea, the others were horrified.

The television company wanted a decision so I gave them Imelda's number to call him directly so that any misunderstandings wouldn't be construed as my fault.

After they rang him, they rang me and said they were thinking of getting him a *skip.* I hyperventilated: if there was *one* thing *guaranteed* to make him change his mind it was the mention of the word "skip". I strongly suggested they not only didn't get a skip, they also *never* used the word in his presence. I pointed out that if they booked a skip I'd bet it would go back empty. They shouldn't waste their money. It was a good job they asked me first. If Imelda was asked or persuaded to put one item in a skip he'd break out in a nasty rash; two items and he'd have palpitations; three ~ well he'd probably need another ride in a nice white, green and yellow vehicle with pretty blue lights on top.

I was aware that there could've been negative repercussions: I didn't want the programme to humiliate him. I could see that his reactions would be highly interesting for the viewers, but I didn't want it to be too stressful for him. He was eighty-three by that time after all and I'd already lost one parent to mental issues.

I also had to ensure Ant was OK with it. He lived in the house too and might have been upset by the room being turned upside down and all the film crew being everywhere.

I spent a few sleepless nights wondering what was best for everyone and whether we were doing the right thing. On the plus side perhaps they'd find my Mum's sewing machine and some more of her diaries. On the minus side they might create so much dust I wouldn't be able to go in at all.

I seriously wondered whether the television company's professional clutter clearers would have any effect. Talking through a person's issues may work for some people but I seriously doubted it would work with Imelda. Like gamblers or alcoholics, the sufferer needs to admit to a problem before they can accept help. Imelda genuinely *didn't believe* he had a problem. I thought he may listen politely to them and then at the end ignore them or tell them he'd do it in his own time and then demand the stuff be brought back in. It was only slightly more likely to work than sending a few hunky blokes around with a skip. As for me ~ I doubted *anyone* would've been able to talk him into throwing anything out. In fact, I would've bet on it.

He was stuck in his ways and at eighty three years old I don't think anyone could have changed anything whether their method was talking to him gently, trying to reason with him, trying to get inside his head or trying to beat him with a stick, it wasn't going to work. He'd always been the most stubborn, pig-headed, single-minded and eccentric person I had ever known. He refused to conform or learn about the modern world ~ he called my laptop "the magic lantern". He hadn't a clue how it worked. He didn't understand how many modern things worked. He really didn't want to understand either.

I was really hoping the clutter busting people would sort him out. Maybe he'd even find long-lost things ~ like his hearing aid, though I often suspected he suffered from "selective" deafness. At best this was highly frustrating for his family and friends and at worst embarrassing for him. He'd had a hearing aid about fifteen years before but once it was lost he didn't bother to replace it. He often told me to speak more clearly; oddly, nobody else ever had a problem hearing me. Sometimes the kids and I would have loved to have shared details of our lives with him; the kids tried many times but he was so deaf that frustration prevented it. Of course we would have persevered if he had shown an interest, however his refusal to replace his hearing aid suggested otherwise.

I could say, 'Dad I'm getting married next week.'

He'd say, 'Oh yes. Now, do you want a Radio Times?'

I had no idea when he had heard me and when he hadn't. I never knew if he'd even understood the gist of whatever I was trying to tell him. He had no idea what the kids were doing at school ~ he couldn't hear them telling him. They tried so hard to talk to him but he talked over them and apparently didn't even try to listen.

At Christmas my friend came over for a visit. She asked my husband how his mother was, as she'd been in hospital. He replied that he doubted she'd last much longer because she was in and out of hospital almost weekly. There was a short awkward silence. Then Dad piped up, 'We had a bumper crop of gooseberries this year and still have some in the freezer.' He apparently hadn't heard a word.

I particularly remember one conversation with him:

'Dad, I'm thinking of taking Cameron skiing ~ what do you think?' (Cameron is my son, six at the time).

'What do I think of what?'

'Of me taking Cameron.'

'Where?'

'Skiing.'

'Oh you're going SKIING!'

'Yes ~ I was thinking of taking Cameron.'

'Oh yes.'

'Do you think he is too young?'

'For what?'

'For skiing, Dad.'

'For skiing, Yes, I said, that's nice. Are you going on your own?'

'No Dad. I was going to take Cameron.'

'Take Cameron where?'

Anyone listening to my one-sided phone conversations with Imelda usually ended up howling with laughter. The phone conversations were far worse than live conversations, although on the up-side, I didn't have to tolerate him shoving his ear in my face.

I spoke to Imelda about the television programme. Imelda said he was OK with them filming again and tidying up just as long as they didn't throw anything out, as he was worried they might throw out something valuable. Apparently the clutter clearing people were able to charge £40 an hour because they *knew* what was valuable and what wasn't. Hell, I knew what was valuable and what wasn't and I didn't charge that. Perhaps I was in the wrong job.

I rang the documentary producers and told them I thought their budget would be wasted on these professionals. The producer agreed. The company had refused to reduce the price and given Imelda's mountain, it would've taken a very long time and cost a fortune. The producer said he'd also been looking at a specialist clearance company that specialised in clearing hoarded houses post-mortem, when a house needed to be cleared for probate. This company were able to recognise antiques and documents and they were fast.

I thought that this would be better: I believed talking him through it would have no effect whatsoever. However, if this company was used to clearing for probate they wouldn't have much experience of having an alive-and-kicking resident hindering their every move. They'd need to be prepared for this. Also, "fast" wasn't a phrase I was happy with ~ I wouldn't be able to keep up.

I made the producer *promise* that if Imelda didn't want something to go out then it wouldn't go out. I said I'd do my damndest to make sure as much as possible was taken out ~ smuggled into my car for disposal later or into kindly neighbours' houses or bins, but Imelda had to have the final word or neither he nor I would've been happy. The producer agreed. He gave me the website details of the company and I investigated it and even called them until I was content.

We finally agreed to a plan to clear just the living room on the first day, store it overnight and then bring anything left back the next day.

# Chapter 29

I arrived early on the day before the clear out. Imelda had a hospital appointment and had asked me to take him. Before we left he said he wanted to take a few boxes of paperwork into another room as he didn't want them getting mixed up in the anticipated confusion. I surveyed the living room while Imelda was getting ready. The amount of stuff was *huge*, so big I doubted their ability to conquer it ~ especially in only two days. It all had to come out so that they could film the room empty. Imelda would have an empty room for a whole night, and the next day the kids would come round and he could enjoy seeing his grandchildren in his house and enjoy some time with them. Then, filming would be finished and the stuff would all come back in. I hoped the weather would be dry, although rain was forecast all day.

I took Imelda to his hospital appointment knowing he'd be there at least two hours, and sneaked back to the mountain with the intention of "having a go" in the living room. I hadn't touched this room during the weeks I'd spent there as he'd asked me not to.

The first ten minutes I spent wondering where the hell to start. The next ten minutes I debated whether to even bother. Finally I clambered round the back of a pile of stuff and removed about thirty of my mother's old Open University books from the book-case. My logic was that if I removed them, then any books found during the clear-up could go in the resulting spaces on the shelves.

I also removed an old mirror, thirty plastic dishes, a pile of papers from 2003 and some plastic boxes. I had a good look round. I couldn't see how on earth they were going to clear one room in just one day. I spotted another television in the pile bringing the total in that one room to **eight**. The televisions were all the cathode ray tube types, not modern flat screen ones and I couldn't think of a reason to keep even one of them. It was difficult to give them away, even if they'd been working. Perhaps I should point out Imelda used to work as a television engineer for the BBC so he did have knowledge about fixing them.

I had to leave before Imelda returned home and caught me. He was coming home on the bus ~ he liked to get out and keep mobile and had become used to wearing his back brace. As I left, the rain became torrential, not uncommon for Wales and I only just made it to the car in time. It was so bad I decided not to go to the skip but to head for home instead.

On the way down the main road I saw Imelda getting off the bus. The house was about seven minutes from the bus stop but the rain was hammering down, he had no umbrella and was getting soaked. Oh the dilemma! Under normal circumstances I would've given him a lift of course, but since I was clearing his house without him knowing, he'd have found out because all his stuff was in the back of my car ~ I'd folded down the back seats to get the stuff in. He'd never trust me again and he'd feel uneasy about leaving the house in the future in case I tried it again ~ I would. So I had to let him walk home in the driving rain and if he caught pneumonia I'd be to blame. Thankfully he didn't see me.

I'd also taken a quick peek at his huge council wheelie bins while I was there so I knew whether we'd be able to use them the next day. He'd filled them both with wood again, proving he had no intention whatsoever of throwing anything else away. This was worse than I'd thought. He'd had the chance to throw things out but obviously had no intention of doing so, despite his promise that he would.

Sometimes I felt like giving up and letting him live in his own pigsty, but there was also poor Ant, who lived in the same house to consider.

For the record, I fully expected him to start hoarding again the second the television crew left, although I realised it would take a fair few years to build things back up to their previous level.

The film crew came round in preparation for the big clear out the next day. They wanted some "before" shots. They found the eight televisions, only one of which was in working order, five yellow pages directories, seven cheap plastic kids watches ~ new and wrapped, a plastic skipping rope, a T-shirt ~ new and wrapped for a two year old, five chains for chain saws ~ new and still boxed, a very old picture of my grandfather in a very old glass frame, a half full bottle of Cointreau all sticky and leaking with a new, sealed bottle of whisky, a bottle of vodka also new and unopened and an old toaster ~ in pieces and plug-less. Imelda reasoned he needed a spare toaster at all times although I reminded him he had two spares in the other room and this one was clearly broken. He said it wouldn't take much to repair it. I pointed out a toaster costs about £10 these days. He argued it was about £15. I said that even if it was £15, it would be cheaper to replace it than locate, buy and pay for postage on a spare part. I doubted he'd be able to find a spare part anyway especially as he didn't have internet access. He put the toaster back on the pile.

There were also three boxes of After Eight mints dated 2002 ~ again Imelda, convinced "best before" means "edible for up to fifteen years after", wanted to keep them.

My plan for clear out day was to reduce the bulk of stuff by putting all the loose bits in boxes of the same size so they'd stack better when they came back in and in theory he could sort through them a box at a time which would be easier for him. I estimated it would reduce the bulk by a third.

On the morning of the big day I hoped I'd be able to sort and remove some of the junk as the boxes came out. Luckily it looked as if my weather angel had booked us in some dry weather for the whole day, again. (Thanks Mum!)

I went round early to find Imelda flapping about trying to move stuff to other rooms. With his broken back in a brace, he wasn't supposed to be moving anything. I had to tell him to stop and leave it to the professionals. He was still flapping so I moved some of the stuff I knew would be staying into another room. I asked if he intended to use this opportunity to get rid of some of his eight old tube televisions in the front room.

He snapped at me; 'I can't think about all that now with all *this* going on.' He was referring to the filming.

'Dad, surely now's *the* time to think about this. Why would you need eight televisions? Really, Dad, why? You can only watch one at a time.'

'I need to see what's needed to repair them. It may only be something small.'

'But Dad, even if you do get round to fixing them, you'd need to find the right part and the space to take them apart ~ space that you don't have. Even if you found the part it mightn't work. If you fixed one and it worked, what would you do with it then? There are eight of them Dad, and even if you fixed all eight nobody wants them these days.'

I bought a tube television for the kids to play games on about five years ago. It was huge, heavy and bulky. It cost £12, and I doubted anybody would want anything similar now ~ even for free. I couldn't *give* mine away although it was fully functional ~ I bought a flat screen so I could have more space. Yet in this room there were eight.

'You need more space, Dad. They could take the televisions and dispose of them for you.'

'Don't ask me stupid questions now ~ I thought you were going to help me, not ask stupid questions. What's that you've thrown in the bin?'

'A stack of empty margarine tubs Dad.'

'Well we don't want to throw those out now do we? They're handy to put things in.' He snatched them from me.

I had to go and sit outside the house at that point, before violence ensued.

The television cameramen turned up shortly after that, followed fifteen minutes later by the van with two sturdy clearance chaps. When I first saw the clearance chaps I was a little shocked as they looked to me exactly like the kind of people my mother warned me about. However, after talking to them and meeting them properly I was much happier.

A very big tarpaulin was put on the back lawn so the grass wasn't ruined, which I thought was a nice touch. The men had brought lots of empty boxes, bin bags and recycling bags with them.

They started bringing stuff out and Imelda started flapping. It was difficult for him to be in two places at once, so every time he was wanted for filming I sneaked a bag or two outside to my car. I ended up with about seven full green and black bags in there and a load of cardboard.

The clearance chaps eventually uncovered the living-room carpet which had been feasted on by generations of moths. They put lots of small bits of rubbish left on the floor into bin bags, but I refused to let them throw the bags out. *Nothing* was to go out unless it had been checked personally by me.

Imelda had blamed me for everything that he couldn't find since he came out of hospital. He still blames me although 99% of the stuff he accused me of throwing out has since reappeared.

While I was on the lawn sorting he kept appearing beside me like a shadow and taking things I was sorting out of my hands, including an old, dusty paperback book of my Mum's that I was about to put in the "keep" box. He took it from me and said, 'We don't throw those out do we?' in the most patronising tone I'd ever heard.

I then found an old Post Office savings book and was looking at it to see if the account had been closed ~ it hadn't. He saw it and snatched it from me. 'You can't throw that out ~ that's a bank book.' as if I were a five year old.

I found a pack of eighteen brand new decorating paintbrushes which I showed him following yesterday's discussion about throwing out the old, dusty, greasy one. I said that now he knew he had eighteen new brushes he could throw out the old one.

He said, 'Don't throw those out! They're new.'

Seriously, he was the master of question avoidance. I could ask and he would ignore, twist or change the subject ~ anything but give me a straight answer.

At one point during the filming he must've forgotten the cameras were there and showed his real character, which can be very unpleasant. I closed my eyes and prayed they kept that part in the final cut ~ I didn't want to appear the evil daughter from hell while he played the sweet old man. I just hoped the final edit gave us all a fair trial.

The moving men asked me *why* I was clearing the house. Well I *was* clearing it so he could come out of the hospital. There was nobody else who could or would do it. I was still helping him because I felt I should. That was a stunningly good question though. Why exactly *was* I still clearing the house? I didn't know how long I could keep going unless Imelda's attitude changed. I welcomed the clear out even though it was only temporary, because I hoped it would be the shove he needed to get him clearing the hoard himself.

Once everything was cleared out there was the sofa, breathing for the first time in about twenty-five years, the carpet was showing despite the huge moth-eaten bare patches in the middle. The place was looking good.

They'd almost filled a van with stuff, but had actually only cleared out about a third of the living-room. The space away from the sofa that would be out of camera shot was left as it was and his office, as promised, hadn't been touched. I wasn't able to go in the room due to the dust. Ant vacuumed and dusted and did what he could.

I left that evening with a huge sense of achievement. Imelda could have at least one clear room for a whole night. How would he feel?

I rang him later to find out but there was no reply. I discovered he had gone out that night to some lecture he was interested in.

I didn't find any family heirlooms nor did I find my mother's sewing machine. I'd managed to put many bits in boxes, reducing the bulk by at least a third and had taken a huge load of junk to the skip on the excuse of nipping out to get lunch for everyone.

Having promised not to throw out anything he specifically said not to, all the eight televisions stayed, though things like old plastic yoghurt pots full of rusty paperclips and corks went out. Old cereal packets, catalogues, ancient phone books, old carrier bags, bits of wood, string, ripped paper and small boxes also went.

When I got home all the kids told me I stank of Granddad's house. All my clothes went in the washing machine and I went in the bath with a large glass of wine and a bag of Galaxy Bites.

The plan for the following day was to take the kids round so Imelda could show everyone what a loving granddad he was.

And then ~ *all* the stuff would go back in.

# Chapter 30

On the final day of filming I took the kids to the mountain with me. It had been raining hard all night and I was worried it would rain all day, too. If everything was wet, Imelda's beloved garden would undoubtedly get trashed and this would make him uptight. By the time we arrived, however, it had stopped raining.

Today's perspective would be to show Granddad the potential of a tidy and uncluttered house and to give him a taste of what it could be like to have his grandchildren round while they are still small enough to be children.

When we arrived the kids were held back and told which way to walk into the room so that the cameras could picture their reactions. They all ran in to the room ~ which, of course, they'd never seen clear of junk ~ and were genuinely amazed. They showed Granddad their drawings they'd done and ran to give him a hug. The huge grin on his face was from ear to ear at having them all there sitting on his sofa with him in the middle. I swear even the cameraman had a tear in his eye, although it could've been the dust.

I couldn't stay in the room for long ~ the dust from the disturbance of forty years of rubbish caused my allergies to flare up. I had to go outside into the garden. While they were filming the kids inside, I spoke to the clearance chaps. One of the removal men gave me £32.78 they'd found having fallen out of the bottom of some boxes. He genuinely apologised and said he now understood why I wouldn't let them throw *anything* out until I'd checked it first!

Over a tea break they mentioned they'd seen a *lot* worse than Imelda's house. Their tales brought me some hope ~ although they'd been used to clearing houses without the owner being there overshadowing every move, they'd fitted in well with the plans that day and they'd been flexible and respectful towards Imelda, for which I was grateful. I wouldn't have been receptive to those "specialist clutter clearance" people who simply "talk" a hoarder through getting rid of their hoard. I'd seen these in hoarder documentaries. Their approach could only work with people who had initiated the procedure and actually wanted to be clear of clutter.

In this instance it was me who initiated it, through writing my (cathartic) blog. I think Imelda would've been quite happy to have lived out the rest of his days in his own personal pigsty had fate not intervened.

Having seen his performance the day before I was sure Imelda would've argued his case with *anyone* who questioned him. Of course any (male) professional would have had an advantage over me in that Imelda would have treated them as fully functioning adults. I was still sore about their charges ~ *forty quid* an hour. Hell, I wished I earned that! My job as a Customer Service Manager involved taking bucket loads of abuse and attitude from people I'd never met: they sometimes spoke to me and my colleagues as if we were moronic amoebas. They whinged and screamed vile abuse at me for such trivial matters it beggared belief.

I'd seen the clutter clearers at work on other hoarding documentaries. The usual format was they talked gently and never judged. They might have suggested, for example, that a person would not need *eight* televisions! They'd ask why the person might possibly have *wanted* eight televisions. They'd ask the person what was the worst that could happen should one of those televisions become lost or stolen. They suggested the person considered how much more space they'd have if one of the televisions wasn't there. All very interesting, but if the person didn't want to get rid of a television then they wouldn't get rid of it.

The junk from the previous day was almost all back in when I suddenly remembered that three years before, Imelda had acquired a huge conference-sized flat-screen computer television as bankruptcy stock when one of the companies he had shares in had folded. The thing was enormous and extremely heavy. Ironically, due to the junk in his house ~ including his eight tube televisions, he'd not been able to fit this new, state-of-the-art television in his house!

He'd managed to persuade his neighbour to store it in his garage. The neighbour had agreed as he had a double garage but had made it clear he was not responsible for it. Wales is famous for its monsoon rainfall and this Welsh garage had no heating and the television was highly likely to have become damp. Imelda must have been aware of this although the day he put it in the garage he told the neighbour it would be only a few days while he cleared a space in the house.

I suggested he asked the moving chaps to bring it in because this was his chance to have a modern TV in his house and a very nice one too. From the way two burly chaps were struggling to lift just the *stand* into the house, it was obviously extremely heavy. The TV must have been about a 48" screen, when it came in we plugged it in and switched it on but it was totally dead. Imelda now had *nine* broken televisions in his house.

The shape of the junk pile changed when it came back in. Instead of being about twenty feet long by about four feet high, the hoard was now about ceiling height by about ten feet wide. There was no room for the mega TV or its stand so they were put in the walkway with a view to moving them later. No one was sure where they were supposed to be moving to or who was going to carry them there but there was nowhere else for them to go. One of the armchairs that had been taken out was brought in last and there was no room for it so it had to go on its side. Logically one would suppose either the chair or the sofa should go out so that the space could be used ~ nobody was realistically going to use them for the purpose of actually sitting in. This would never happen.

At about 4:00 the camera crew had finished and all the stuff was back in the house, they had a quick cup of tea and said they'd need to get going as the skies were an ominous grey. While the cameraman was getting in his car the first drops of rain started and within ten minutes of everyone leaving, the rain was coming down in torrents. We went back inside; the sofa was clear but for three large black bags of bits of rubbish from the floor containing what appeared to be rubbish ~ scrunched up used tissues, bits of string, paper clips, corks, broken pencils, old Christmas cards, bits of wood etc. Even so, they all had to be sorted. The bags were placed "temporarily" on the newly reclaimed sofa. I asked Imelda if he wanted me to take one bag home and sort it. He said he didn't, because he hadn't even looked through them yet. I said that sorting out was exactly what I was offering to do *for* him. He replied that he wanted to look through it first and generously said that I could have it once this was done if I liked. How thoughtful!

Earlier on I'd also carefully sorted a bagful of what was, to my personal satisfaction, total rubbish. He came over to check it out.

'What's that you've got?'

'It's all sorted, Dad, and it's all rubbish. Really it is ~ you can check if you like but honestly, I've sorted it really carefully. Dad. Look, you have to trust me at some point!'

His reply was, 'Yes, but I'd like to see, just in case ~ you may not have *deliberately* thrown things out and I know you *think* you're helping...' He took the bag from me and opened it. He rummaged through the contents and removed a stick of splintery wood, a bit of thick flexi-plastic about 10cm square, a plastic curtain hook and a paper clip, presumably just to prove to me just how totally inept I was at sorting through bins ~ or maybe just because he felt it necessary. I don't know, but I do know I had to walk away clenching my fists and biting my lip.

# Chapter 31

Three days after the filming I visited Imelda and noticed that all the black bins from all the other houses were outside in the street awaiting the weekly council rubbish collection. I told him that the bin lorry was at the bottom of the road.

'Ah, um, I've some waste I need them to take.'

*This,* I thought, *is going to be interesting.* I asked if he needed help getting the bin outside, but he didn't answer, this in itself wasn't unusual. Instead, he hobbled outside, where the bin lorry was reversing up the road.

I then witnessed an amazing transformation. Imelda donned his "Damsel in Distress" act, hobbling to the bin man with his best "my back is broken" walk ~ which was odd because by then he was walking perfectly well. Smiling sweetly all his frown lines turned to smiles and he could fool anybody ~ except me, that is. Then, in his "poor old man" voice he asked the bin man, 'Would you mind awfully if I gave you a bag of acorns? If you give me a minute I'll just go into the garden and get them, though it may take a while though, because as you see, I've broken my back.' A pathetic expression swept over his face. He deserved an Oscar.

'Ah,' said the bin man, showing great concern, 'don't you worry there Sir, I'll get them for you.' With a cheery smile he followed Imelda to his back garden, from whence, about two minutes later he reappeared staggering under the weight of an *enormous* black bag full of acorns. Imelda waltzed down the path after him, a huge smile on his face.

Exactly how did Imelda collect the big bag of acorns? I suspect he enlisted Ant's assistance. He was certainly doing more lifting and clearing than he should have, despite his back-brace. Of course, collecting acorns was a matter of supreme urgency, far more important than clearing the house because if they weren't collected immediately they'd root and grow into thirty foot oak trees overnight.

Why didn't he use the council provided green wheelie bin specifically designed for garden waste? Because it was full of bits of wood for the fire, that's why. Why didn't he use the council-provided black wheelie bin for general household rubbish? Because that too was full of bits of wood for the fire. For the record the small brown council food waste bin was also full, of you guessed it, bits of wood for the fire and was sitting neatly next to the fireplace.

So, where *did* he put his rubbish for collection? He didn't appear to have any rubbish for collection, which was odd, because only days before he had a team of clearance men, two cameramen, Ant and me in the house specifically to help clear the mountains of junk he'd accumulated over the past thirty or so years. You'd have thought he would've had at least a crisp packet to dispose of, but apparently not!

Could it possibly be ~ no surely not! Could it be that, that ~ Hell no, could it, I mean it couldn't ~ could it? Could it be that now he has newly exposed space in his house he's going to accumulate *more* stuff?

No ~ surely not!

# Chapter 32

I decided I'd give myself a break from the mountain for a while to recover, enjoy my own family ~ and because I felt I was going just a little bit insane. I'd begun to remember the negative health effects I used to have from living with that level of junk. I'd suffered with far more than my fair share of medical ailments in the allergy spectrum while I'd been growing up in that house. Over the past few weeks both my asthma and eczema had flared up, despite me taking antihistamines, wearing dust protection and showering as soon as I got home each day.

Allergies to dust, cobwebs, animal fur, whatever, make asthma and eczema worse. Dust causes itching skin and constant sneezing. Constant scratching of the maddening irritation makes the skin bleed, with the likelihood of consequent skin infections and ugly scars. Skin thickens from scarring and gradually loses its ability to stretch and to regulate body temperature, so as a result the sufferer is unable to tolerate heat and equally, suffers much more from cold than a person with normal skin. Because the skin's normal temperature regulation doesn't work then the person may become hot when others are cold or cold when others are hot and going out in the sun will cause the skin to look like a Dalmatian in negative as the scars don't tan. It's sometimes likened to the skin being a size too small.

For fifteen years I refused to wear a t-shirt because I was embarrassed about my red itchy, scabby, scarred skin and bloodstains. I refused to apply for jobs which required a short sleeved uniform, and as a result my confidence took a huge hit. I couldn't look people in the eye. When I went shopping in summer I wore fingerless gloves because every time a shop assistant put change in my hand I saw the look of horror on their faces.

Eventually, I wrote an article for the National Eczema Society magazine and GMTV got in touch and asked me to go on Lorraine Kelly's morning programme. They paid for me to see a Harley Street doctor who believed in alternative medicine, who gave me a diet to follow ~ dairy and gluten and wheat free. After about six weeks I saw the doctor again and appeared again on the Lorraine Kelly show in a tee-shirt. It was a very proud moment for me as it was the first time in fifteen years I'd worn a tee-shirt in public. Amazing!

The diet treatment worked, but the diet was very restrictive and so I stopped following it. Coincidentally, at about the same time I moved into my own flat and the eczema was never quite as bad from then on although, interestingly, after I've been to Imelda's house clearing up I need a soak in the bath to stop it flaring up again.

When my skin was clear, my confidence improved 100% and I'm a *very* different person now.

I saved the worst ~ asthma ~ until last. My doctor explained that the more severe attacks I had, the more chance there was of my lungs becoming scarred. Scarred lungs are very bad. I was hospitalised so many times due to asthma attacks I'd lost count. Asthmatic children are so desperate to fit in that they will try to play down their condition, but this doesn't help because if assistance isn't prompt during an attack the asthma can't be controlled. I know now that there were many, many times I should have seen a doctor and one or two when I should have had an ambulance but instead I kept quiet and struggled through. God! I wish now I'd had the confidence then to have asked someone to call an ambulance.

Because of the hoard I didn't often invite school friends home. It was embarrassing and I didn't know how to explain it. I was already teased due to my skin ~ I didn't want to be teased for living in a pigsty as well. So I went to my friends' houses. The problem was most of them had pets and I've always been sensitive to animal hair. I was (and still am) highly allergic to house dust (house dust mite) and *all* furry animals ~ cats, dogs, rabbits, mice, gerbils, guinea pigs and horses.

I'd try to pretend I was OK, but clearly I wasn't and within minutes of entering their house I'd be struggling to breathe. When this happened it was difficult to talk so I'd be silent. I'm sure my friends' parents thought of me as the quiet and shy little asthmatic girl with the itchy skin. I was so trapped at that time. There was nowhere I could be the real me and be free of the allergies until, as I've already mentioned, I went to work in the ski resorts, when I had four whole months free of asthma and eczema every year.

I remember a particularly severe attack, though I'm not sure if it was the same one that resulted in me being on a ventilator or a different one. There were so many.

I was struggling so hard to breathe, terrified that I was going to die. The attack had happened very quickly and none of my inhalers were working. I needed help and I needed an ambulance, fast. I hated to make a fuss but I knew I was in serious jeopardy. I was in my bedroom watching my small TV while Dad went downstairs to call an ambulance. Mum was sitting with me. The ambulance took so long. I remember the start music of a programme on my small bedroom television and asking Mum to turn it down so I could hear the ambulance. I sat stiff with fear and concentrated on just getting enough oxygen into my lungs to stay conscious until the ambulance arrived. I couldn't allow myself to panic. It felt as if the ambulance would never come.

The programme finished and still there was no ambulance, which was odd ~ a 22 year old with a severe asthma attack in the middle of a major city only five minutes from the hospital, yet the ambulance had already taken half an hour. Imelda appeared shortly after the programme finished, obviously having been watching it on the bigger television set downstairs.

He asked if I was better yet. I managed to find the breath to ask him to find out when the ambulance would come, and he said, 'Well, I suppose I had better call them then if you really need one.'

I realised he hadn't yet telephoned, but had decided to leave me for a while to see how it went *after* I had asked him to call the ambulance. I'd never call the emergency services unnecessarily and, had I not been convinced I was about to run out of oxygen permanently, wouldn't have bothered them. Imelda was playing God with me and deciding for himself when it was appropriate to call.

When it dawned on me that I'd have to wait even longer I almost gave up and passed out with fear. I made a desperate last ditch attempt to get air by launching myself off the (horsehair) mattress towards the open window. I think this spooked him, because then, and only then, did he call the ambulance.

In the throes of a serious asthma attack, it's difficult to speak ~ any energy is taken up in trying to breathe ~ to survive. Once the ambulance was finally called they arrived really quickly and I was taken out of the hellhole for a few days of clean air in hospital. I wondered many times if my father really cared about me. Surely, if he did then he would've done something about the mess which was causing my problems.

Then, I didn't fully realise the extent of my mother's suffering and how hard she constantly battled to get rid of the squalor in which she was forced to live. I didn't know how many times she'd visited neighbours for a break ~ and to put rubbish in their bins. I was unaware how hard she must have battled with him to keep the place decent. It must have killed her to see her children's health suffering and not be able to do anything about it.

# Chapter 33

When I was small, my paternal grandparents lived in a big house in South Wales, with a lovely garden to play in. it had lots of trees and a railway track at the bottom that fascinated Ant and me. At Easter we'd go there for the annual egg hunt, although I don't remember much about the inside of the house because, as kids, we weren't allowed inside. This was, according to my mother, because my grandmother was herself an extreme hoarder. I don't remember what she kept but there was a lot of it.

Imelda's father 'Pops' was almost at the other end of the spectrum, and when Imelda's mother died he moved into a much smaller two bed flat which was always immaculate. He was so house proud and he became somewhat stressed when we kids put all our stuff all over the place when we visited. He also had a garage that was empty ~ he put his car inside! Imagine that! A garage with space for a car! He rid himself of almost everything his wife had hoarded over a lifetime. That proves it is possible so there's hope for me yet.

When Pops died, Imelda was the only remaining son and so he inherited *all* of the contents of his father's flat. I found a lot of it when I was clearing his house. Pops died in about 1980 so Imelda has had over thirty years to sort through it. It's still waiting. The boxes it all came in are still in Imelda's bedroom and attic.

So Imelda's mother was a hoarder, then Imelda... Does that mean it now passes to me? I sincerely hope not. I think many families of hoarders, once they leave home, are overly tidy to compensate for the confusion and havoc in which they've grown up. My family think I am a bit overprotective of the vacuum. It's *my* vacuum cleaner and I like to use it all the time. At risk of sounding somewhat odd, I find it therapeutic to empty the dust out and to clean the filters.

There ~ my secret's out. I think I'm fairly normal, apart from the vacuum thing. My mates may disagree, they describe me as "a bit individual ~ but in a nice way". I think that's good. I have a pet corn snake who lives in a tank in my living room, but other than that I seem to have got off fairly lightly on the weird front. The kids make a mess, as all kids do but that is OK and always cleaned up again in a few days. The kids' bedrooms are usually chaotic. My twins share a room. One half is very tidy and the other ~ well I suspect *if* the hoarding gene is going mutate anywhere it may well be there.

I understand that OCD can be an issue in hoarder families and I admit to checking that the gas is off, the television is not on standby, the doors are locked and the snake's cage doors are closed, perhaps a few too many times before I go to bed. I figure this is just being careful.

I saw a friend's parents in the local supermarket recently. Her mother asked how the kids were, and how my dad was ~ she'd heard about his fall. She'd also seen the blog, but until reading it, hadn't realised the true extent of the issue. Their house is gorgeous inside ~ white carpets, masses of space and very clean and tidy. It's spacious, clutter free and kept very clean and therefore really relaxing to be in. It's everything I would love in a house. They had it built about fifteen years ago to their specifications. I imagined myself visiting my parents with my kids in a house like that. Perfect!

Sadly, that's never going to happen. It's such a shame Imelda's house is the way it is. The green sofa is almost fifty years old, flattened to within an inch of its life, eaten by moths and it smells musty and old. I perch on the edge of it if I have to sit down at all. The carpet has a vile, seventies horror of an orange flower pattern on it where the moths haven't eaten it. If only Imelda had some pride in his house, it has the potential to be gorgeous. His next door neighbours also have the same style houses and I've been in both: they're lovely, relaxing, quiet, spacious and clean ~ houses I'd be proud to own. Then there is Imelda's, right in the middle. A thorn between two roses...

Mum was very house-proud and loved to do homey stuff like cooking and sewing, and she worked to keep the house looking stunning too ~ at first. It would have been the house of her dreams had it not been for the total chaos and neglect inside. I simply can't imagine what it must be like to have to live with that level of increasing havoc.

I finished reading her diaries recently and they tell of her constant battle with Imelda and his junk. Oddly, in my own rediscovered teenage diaries, I hadn't mentioned the junk much at all; possibly I considered my home to be normal. However, I noticed an alarming number of diary entries of me going into hospital with chronic asthma or severe eczema and I spent most of my childhood on steroids and wrapped in cream and bandages. Perhaps at the time, that was also normal.

My mother must have been desperate by then, watching her daughter suffer in that way and not being able to do anything about it. I'm almost sure she must have had some form of slow mental breakdown. There were small signs back then which I can only recall with hindsight. I'm sure anyone would suffer mental issues trying to raise a family whose health was deteriorating in that level of clutter and dust, and all while working full time as an English teacher in a high school.

I still can't visit Imelda without wearing a dust mask; he says he can't understand what I'm saying with 'that stupid thing' on my face. His gratitude and sympathy are just overwhelming sometimes!

~

I recently read an article in a women's magazine: *"Ways to clear clutter".* I suspect this type of article is usually just an attempt to sell something, but I figured I'd read it anyway, if only for my own amusement:

1) *Do you have a narrow hall?* He does. The article says hallways can fill up with coats and jackets and it suggests a wall rack. Good plan! Except if he bought a rack it would add to the junk for five plus years until (if ever) he got round to fitting it. Oh, he'd also need to be able to reach the wall.

2) *Most of us have more shoes than we ever wear.* No s**t Sherlock! It says that once you've whittled down the stash to a sensible level, you should store them in a cabinet. "Whittled down to a sensible level" ~ what the heck does *that* mean? It suggests a rack which can hold up to ten pairs. OK... So ~ what about the other 177 shoes?

3) *Don't let bills and letters get lost ~ file them in a letter rack.* That would need to be about 6ft x 4ft.

4) *Let wellies drip dry out of the way on a rack.* ~ You try finding a space anywhere near a wall to hang a welly rack. If there were such a rack it would be full of papers and letters which had overflowed from the letter rack.

5) *Christmas decorations stored in transparent boxes under the stairs are easy to find.* Yes, I'm sure they would be if you could actually reach the cupboard under the stairs, and open the door in the first place. Imelda has his very own solution to this one ~ keep the decorations and fairy lights up all year round and only switch the lights on at Christmas. A fantastic solution, not only do you not have to find anywhere to store them, but you can just build up your card collection year after year and so it looks like you have lots of friends.

6) *Know where your keys are by storing them in this colourful key storage box.* Er ~ I think he'd lose the box before it got as far as the wall.

7) *A nice environment is important to getting restful sleep and your bedroom should feel like a sanctuary. Keep your room free from junk and clutter particularly the space around your bed.* You don't say! So where exactly do you put the five feet high piles of junk mail, newspapers, old chairs, slippers, boxes and other stuff? Where do you put the hundreds of newspapers which have already started to creep onto your bed, because there's no room for them on the piles on the floor? Clearing a space round his bed took me two days and that was with four friends helping.

8) *Take advantage of the space beneath the bed.* Space?

9) *Try on the contents of your wardrobe; donate the reject pile to charity including anything which needs altering as the chances are it won't get done.* Well, the last bit hit the nail on the head but ~ "reject pile"? Oh and of course you have to be able to get to the wardrobe and to open the doors first.

10) *A storage coffee table.* Excellent idea ~ until there's so much stuff on top that you can't see the table let alone open the lid. Whatever's inside is then lost for ever.

11) *TVs are getting slimmer but larger.* Imelda take note! It suggests saving space by hanging them on the wall. Can you do that with box type TVs? Er – would that be all *nine* of them in the living room?

12) *Ornaments – Less is more!* Never a truer word spoken.

13) *Organise drawers with handy drawer organisers.* (These wouldn't fit in the house let alone the drawers).

14) *Check the medicine cabinet regularly.* This means at least every twenty years judging by Imelda's cabinet.

15) *Use every bit of the kitchen to best advantage planning storage right up to the ceiling.* Oh dear God! No! Please don't encourage him.

16) *Tallboys save space as they take up less floor space.* Unless there isn't enough floor space to get one in the house.

17) *Don't forget to clean out the spare room.* The article says according to a recent survey, 80% of people couldn't list more than five items they had stored in their spare room. Neither could Imelda but it doesn't mean he can't think of an excuse to keep more.

18) *Shoes will last longer if they are cared for properly.* Ahem! It suggests shoe storage boxes with windows in. All very well ~ unless you have 197 odd shoes and no room for boxes.

I don't know if it's a girl thing or just me, but I love to buy new things, move things around and change my surroundings every now and then. I also enjoy throwing things out, having the space the old thing's absence has created. Then I like to fill it with new, more modern stuff. No living in the past for me. I like new, I like white, I like fresh and I like clean. I enjoy throwing stuff in a skip and the feeling of out with the old and in with the new.

Imelda doesn't share that gene.

# Chapter 34

I have no idea if hoarding typically extends to cars. If you have a hoarding tendency do you keep your car clean and tidy because people are far more likely to see it in the car park or do you keep as much stuff in your car as you do in your house?

I've read articles which advise that the more weight you keep in your car the more fuel the car will use. My last car ~ a Renault Laguna ~ had a huge boot and I used it to store many things. I concealed the kids' Christmas presents in it for about a month. I had three packets of Galaxy Bites in there ~ emergency rations ~ because if I took them inside they wouldn't survive the hour. One never knows when one will be caught short where Galaxy Bites are concerned. I kept my hi-viz bike jacket there, a pair of wellies, a few umbrellas, a storage box, a cushion, a blanket and a bucket, all locked in the boot out of sight.

Oggy, my current little Toyota Rav4 has about enough boot space for a lipstick, a packet of Galaxy Bites and a set of jump leads. No place to store anything. Whenever I filled her for the skip run I had to fold the back seats down.

Imelda has a Ford Focus with a decent size boot and a lot of "stuff" in it. It isn't any one kind of "stuff" ~ it's just "stuff" in general. The poor car was stuck on Imelda's drive because he wasn't allowed to drive after he broke his back. He would soon be allowed to drive again, so he had it serviced and a brand new MOT put on it. For sure the garage saw him coming because they charged him £800 to get the thing through the MOT ~ the car is probably worth £350 top. A 2002 dark green Ford Focus full of junk. The log book says it's *silver* but since it hasn't been cleaned in a while it's grown an interesting layer of mossy wildlife. Imelda argues this is because his drive is north facing. I think it's more to do with a lack of application of soap and water for the past five years. It needs a scraper rather than a sponge and would benefit from a trip to the jet wash.

Last summer at 3am I had to take Imelda and Ant to the airport for their holiday to Spain. I'd offered to take them ~ the traffic at that time of day is virtually non-existent so I figured, airport, home, back to bed. Simples!

Imelda turned up at my house late, as usual, in the Focus, which also smells of wet dog and "eau de feet". What can I say? The thing is bogging and I am glad it was dark. We got to the airport and I dropped him off. I then discovered I didn't have a £1 coin to get out of the drop-off zone. There was a coin bin system so it had to be a coin. I had to faff about in the dark looking for loose coins as the inside light was broken. Eventually, I parked the car up and ran through the car park in the rain looking like a bedraggled rat until I managed to find someone with change.

Eventually I left the airport ~ behind someone who was apparently driving a wheeled wardrobe, although I believe it may have been a car. The driver was unfortunately a member of the "10mph less than the speed limit" club. Typical, only two vehicles on the road that time of day and I am forced to do 40 in a 50mph zone. In Oggy or on the bike I'd have been gone, but in the green Focus I wasn't going to pull any fancy stuff. Between the airport and Cardiff runs a long, 50mph road, nice and twisty that used to be great for biking, but a few years ago it was used as an experiment for the "Let's see how many roundabouts we can fit on one stretch of road" project. I was stuck behind Mr "10mph less", doing forty, slowing down to twenty for each roundabout.

I rapidly got bored, frustrated and hungry, not a good mix for a tired driver so I looked for a solution. Suddenly, out of the haze, like a mirage in the desert ~ a huge Tesco Extra appeared, all lit up and beckoning to me. I figured I'd lose Mr 10mph below, get a bite to eat and a drink and dammit, I could finally say I'd been shopping at 4am. I parked the Focus in a dark part of the car park ~ for fear of someone seeing me get out and thinking it was mine and strode into Tesco. I found a bottle of orange juice, a nice croissant and a packet of wine gums and smugly headed for the only open checkout. I smiled at the checkout girl who looked at me a bit gone off. *She must be bored,* I thought. Then I realised that I was wearing my penguin pyjamas ~ in the middle of Tesco, and as if that wasn't bad enough, I was wearing them with cowboy boots! Heck! That was even worse than driving a green Ford Focus!

There was a big thing in the papers a year or so back about people shopping in Tesco in their pyjamas and I remember discussing these disgraceful slobs at work with my colleagues.

I made a swift exit and continued home. Back on familiar roads and singing loudly to the Pet Shop Boys (as you do), I saw a bright blue light in my rear view mirror. *"Aye aye,"* I thought, *"someone's for it."* Yes, they were ~ flipping me, again. Maybe it was a case of bored policeman syndrome or possibly it was due to me looking somewhat nervous (about being recognised in a green Focus). He pulled me over for a "quick chat" and asked me a few questions as I tried to hide my pyjamas. Then he let me go.

Finally I got back home, my penguin PJs smelling nicely of feet and wet-dog and parked the Focus two streets away where it could wait for the return journey a fortnight later.

After two days I had a rush of blood to the head and decided to wash the thing for him. It was a nice sunny day and I got out there with the toothbrush, hot soapy car shampoo and the hosepipe. Two hours later I'd managed to get the shrubbery off it. I then got the polish out and did my very best. After a further hour it looked passable as a car. I was proud of my efforts.

During the week I attacked the inside of it as well and was rather chuffed with the result when I went to collect him from the airport at 2pm. The car gleamed in the bright afternoon sun. Imelda didn't even notice!

Now it's green and abandoned and full of stuff again, and I wonder if this will also happen to the house after all my efforts this summer. We'll have to wait and see.

While Imelda was in hospital, the doctors noticed he was hard of hearing and he was seen by an audiologist. He'll be getting a new hearing aid shortly. It will be wonderful if he can start to be part of the family again by showing he wants to hear what we're saying.

As I've mentioned, he's always suffered from selective deafness, and though I've become used to it, it infuriates me when he ignores the kids, who like most kids have very clear and loud, high pitched voices. They talk to him and he completely ignores them. On many occasions he's been sitting in my kitchen and one of the children will start talking to him. He'll initially acknowledge them ~ but then he loses interest, forgets they're speaking because he can't hear them and often gets up and walks away mid-conversation, which upsets both them and me. They mostly don't bother talking to him anymore.

I guess I'll never know the real reason for his refusal to replace his hearing aid when he lost it fifteen years ago. Perhaps he was too embarrassed to tell the doctor he'd lost it although I don't think this was the reason. As a result I don't think he's ever had a whole conversation with any of the children. I don't think he knows what they like or don't like, or what they do in school or who their friends are or anything. It irritates me that he can't even *pretend* to be interested.

My children are losing interest in him, their only surviving grandparent. Every time they try to engage him in conversation it's always one sided.

It was much the same when I was little. He was of the very old fashioned "Children should be seen and not heard" mind-set. He'd frequently tell me to 'Stop yapping!' or loudly 'SHHHH!' me if he was watching something on TV. He'd do it to all of us ~ including my Mum ~ right up until I left home and beyond. I eventually stopped bothering to try to involve him in anything I was doing.

A "Eureka!" moment, when the possibility that I was actually a fully functioning adult with a mind and life of my own, hit him years later. The realisation that his own daughter had something to say which was actually *interesting* and that she was even possibly capable of holding an adult conversation didn't come until I was 25 or so.

In about 1990, the company he worked for were offering weekend courses in London aimed at giving retirement age staff information about their forthcoming retirement. Mum was ill by then and not able to go, so I went instead.

Imelda had gone up to get breakfast and I was sitting at the breakfast table at the hotel. A senior colleague of his, also on the course, came over and asked to join us. We began talking about America where he said he was going in a few weeks for the first time ever. As I'd been to America a few years previously I was telling him what I'd seen and what to expect on his forthcoming trip. The colleague listened to me with genuine interest and we were deep in conversation when Imelda returned with his cornflakes.

He sat down politely and saw his senior colleague listening with obvious interest to me. He listened as he munched and the lights came on in his head. This was his senior colleague, engaged in an adult conversation, which was *interesting,* with another adult ~ who was his very own daughter! It was a total revelation. He kept saying to me, 'you never told me that!' and 'I never knew that!', though I'd talked to him about my US adventures many, many times over the years since my return, but he'd never bothered to listen to me. In his eyes I was still only a child.

~

If I have some spare time, I make various craft items, my speciality being small, one of a kind teddy-bears. My friend and I take a stall together at local craft fairs, it keeps us busy and we get out and meet like-minded crafty people. Sometimes we even sell something!

We're currently making sock animals ~ mainly monkeys. They're brightly coloured and popular and because they're handmade they're all different with individual appeal. Whenever I'm shopping I buy socks. Wild, wacky, zany, cheap and cheerful socks ~ and then I "sock animal" them. However, it takes time to work through them all, and I have a stockpile of boxes of socks. They sell very fast, but I am still buying faster than I can convert them. When my friend saw my stock, she accused me of being a sock hoarder! The "H" word horrified me. Was she right?

Now, I don't see sock hoarding as an issue, but then Imelda doesn't see *his* hoarding as an issue, either. I agree, I have a lot of socks, but then there are five people with ten feet between them living in my house so they'll all get used even if I don't turn them into monkeys or aliens. For once I'm busy doing something other than clearing junk and I'm enjoying it.

~

Imelda has now been given the go ahead to drive his car and he has his independence back. He visited us yesterday for the first time since he'd fallen in August. He trudged through the house. The kids had left a pile of drawings on the floor by the armchair. Imelda stood on them. This upset the kids and they asked him to get off. Despite the state of his house, when he comes to mine he seems to assume that if something is on the floor he has every right to step on it. He'd walk into my living room and *crack!* One of the kid's toys bit the dust. He'd say, 'Well it was on the floor!' as if that made it all ok.

In my average sized house, over 95% of the floor is visible. It may not be the tidiest house in the world but it's not the untidiest either. It is a normal urban house with a family of five living in it. There's lots of floor to walk on.

I said 'Dad, please could you get off? You're standing on the kids' drawings.' He totally overdid the "Oh my goodness, am I standing on something?" bit, and made a big act of getting off.

Then he said, "Well, if it's on the floor it's going to get trodden on isn't it?'

Now, I'm not asking for an award for not shooting him, but Hell, he tries my patience!

# Chapter 35

For a month or so after Imelda came home from hospital I rarely went to his house. I delayed going to the mountain to see how he got on by himself. Would he clear anything? Would he get rid of the armchair that was lying on its side in the living room because it wouldn't fit upright? Would he clear the kitchen so that he could fit a bread roll on the worktop? Would he sort out his hundreds of odd shoes? Would he move the eleven-boxes-high tower from in front of the cupboard under the stairs so he could find my winter coat, which is so old it's vintage. Would he sort through the three black bags of bits that had been sitting on the sofa for weeks?

After a while I went round to visit. His green garden waste council wheelie bin was full of wood bits again. Despite the council only accepting rubbish in the black wheelie bin for collection, Imelda's black bin remained full of bits of wood.

The three large bin bags filled with stuff they'd picked up off the floor during the filming were still on the sofa, which had quite clearly not been used for its original purpose since the film crew left. The bags would only have taken me twenty minutes to sort, but there was *another* box on top of the bags and another in front.

I decided I'd give him a further month to get sorted, and then I planned to sneak in and remove a few bits, like an old bathroom plastic chair/storage stool from my granddad's flat which remained in Imelda's bedroom. It hadn't been used for about twenty years, it was empty, the plastic was split and the nasty, blue polyester fur on top was thick with dust and age. It was occupying space in his bedroom.

My plan was to *find* it, and then do the "*Oh my goodness that is just what a friend in a new house has been looking for. That would go perfectly in her bathroom,*" routine.

Imelda would do the, *"Well if you really like it I suppose I could let you have it"* act, for which I would have to feign extreme gratitude.

Then, smiling gratefully, I'd take it to my car and drive away with a cheery wave of thanks for extra effect, depositing the vile item at the council recycling centre on the way home.

It was a well-worn routine. Imelda believed he was doing me a favour by letting me have some beloved and well-used possession. I pretended to be ecstatic at my good fortune or at how thrilled I was that it was exactly what my friend was looking for. I donated it to 'Skip' and everyone was happy.

While passing one day, I popped in to get a nice small branch from his garden for my pet snake to climb on. His garden had lots and lots of wood. I explained what I was after and set off to find it. He watched me like a hawk. I found the perfect piece, about a foot long with some nice climbing bits shooting off from it, and turned to leave. Imelda blocked my path.

'What's that for?' as if it was his best and only piece of wood!

'For Trouser to climb on Dad!'

'Oh! Well yes, I suppose you can take that one!'

I wasn't quite sure what that was about, since he had enough wood to heat the Albert Hall for this Millennium and probably half the next, yet he was upset because I'd taken *one small piece of cut tree branch* for my pet snake!

# Chapter 36

I'd read a few books on hoarding and noted, apart from the stress of living with clutter, reduced living space, embarrassment, worry and the constant search for buried items, there were other factors which commonly affected members of a family who lived with a hoarder. Often the family noted there were medical conditions which had a common theme and I suspected a common cause. Allergies were regularly mentioned as were skin issues and breathing problems.

I'd had the health issues since I was three, following my first hospital admission. I was told they were caused by an atopic condition and that I'd grow out of them. However they got worse, not better. I couldn't do sports in school because I couldn't breathe. The school decided asthmatics should be treated normally. This was fine, except that against all those competitive, sporty types I clearly didn't measure up.

Outdoor games were a nightmare because as well as the asthma, there was the eczema and apart from the visual part, there was the skin temperature regulation problem.

When you're a kid nobody tells you the side effects, long term effects or possible causes of medical conditions. Kids just get on with life. When you're only a kid, if the doctors have time to explain anything, they tell your parents, not you. Often the doctor treats the symptoms not the cause ~ sometimes they don't even know the cause. In my case only with hindsight do I know what the cause was. That cause was there since I was born and remains there to this day.

My mother, of course, would have done anything in her power for me, but she was helpless because of the extreme levels of dust in the house.

Doctors and allergy specialists suggested various methods to help sufferers. Firstly they said the dust levels should be kept down by vacuuming regularly and damp dusting all surfaces daily. This was pretty obvious, providing the vacuum cleaner could be found. Once it was found, the floor also needed to be found. As for the dusting ~ imagine a nice clear shelf: one swipe and it's done. Now imagine the same shelf with piles and piles of stuff on it. Imagine that on every shelf and every surface in every room.

Specialists also suggested vacuuming the mattress daily. However, as soon as the sheets and quilt were moved, all the dust in the rest of the room took flight.

In summer, they suggested, keeping all doors and windows closed to control ingress of pollen. That was the only chance of fresh air we had!

*Have floorboards instead of carpets* they said. Great idea ~ once you could *find* the carpet to remove it.

Keep clutter to a minimum. Er ~ Right!

~

Nowadays my skin is clear and I wear whatever I like and apart from the scars, which no longer bother me, I'd say my skin is normal. It didn't recover completely until I was 38, after my son was born. The asthma is still an issue and I still avoid animals. However, now I have the confidence to ask if someone has a dog or cat when they invite me to their house, and I don't visit if they have. They always insist Rover/Tiddles is very clean and doesn't moult, or they promise to put him/her in the garden, but this is useless: traces of fur still lurk and the allergy is now too bad to risk it.

Three years ago I spent Christmas Eve night sleeping in an old people's home because we'd gone to stay with a relative who had two dogs. The dogs had been sent to a friend for the duration, the relative had vacuumed and dusted, but within thirty minutes of arriving I was struggling to breathe. After an hour I had to sit in the car.

After an hour in the car I went to the hospital and was given a nebuliser and steroids and told, "Do NOT go back into that house!" by the doctors. Someone kindly arranged for me to use the bed at the old folk's home in their family room. I couldn't drive home and my kids were all getting on with enjoying their Christmas.

By the time I got a taxi the next morning to join my family in the conservatory of the house, which had the windows open and no carpets, the kids had already opened all their presents. My Christmas was half over and I felt really bad for ruining theirs.

I'd probably have had allergies, asthma and eczema even if I hadn't grown up in a hoarder's house, although I'm the only one of my whole family who has all three to the same extreme extent. I suspect that living with all the dust and the horsehair mattress was at least partly to blame.

I don't go to Imelda's house unless I absolutely have to and then I make it as quick as I can. The minute I walk in the door I have a wild urge to turn and run. The good thing is now I *can* turn and run as I have somewhere to go. I didn't have that luxury when I was a kid.

I went to the house in December as I was about to post off my Christmas cards and I thought I'd help Imelda out by posting his at the same time. I rang him in advance so he'd be ready.

'Hello?'

'Hello Dad. It's me!'

'Me... Hello me. Who is that?'

'Izabelle, Dad ~ your daughter!'

'Who?'

'Me Dad. IT'S ME!'

'Oh, right! I thought you were one of those wretched sales people trying to sell me something...'

'Have you got your hearing aid now Dad?'

'What?'

'Have you got your hearing aid now?'

'What? Have I what? ~ Izabelle is that you?'

That was a *"no"* then! Everyone who knew him had been eagerly awaiting the arrival of the hearing aid so that we could stop speaking in words of one syllable in a mon-o-tone, because anything else had to be repeated many times. If he didn't hear and the sentence had to be repeated, after eight repeats if you should have happened to RAISE YOUR VOICE, he'd shout over you, saying he couldn't hear what you were saying and that you shouldn't shout or he wouldn't be able to hear you. Oh, and that you should also "improve your diction and speak more clearly without rushing".

Once he started on this particular lecture there was no point in repeating yourself or mentioning that if he wore his hearing aid, matters might improve. You could only stand there, desperately restraining yourself from picking up the nearest blunt instrument and clouting him with it. Clearly it was *your* fault he didn't hear you.

Six weeks after he was fitted with his new hearing aid I asked him where it was. He said he hadn't had time to play about with it yet and it was still in the box somewhere. I asked what he'd been doing for six weeks. His explanation was that it was Christmas, although what a retired person needed to do to prepare for Christmas was a mystery.

This brings me back to the cards I was intending to post for him. Each year he intends to send cards but never gets round to it. Last year he brought his family cards round to me on Boxing Day saying it was possibly slightly late but it was better late than never! He says he has *so* much to do it's getting him down.

What? ~ Perhaps he was keeping busy tidying and clearing! ~ Perhaps not.

He asked me if I'd seen a little red plastic egg-timer that he kept in the cupboard and I said I hadn't touched that cupboard. He replied that he hadn't seen it since I'd been messing about. So, all those weeks of me and my friends clearing his bogging house for up to eight hours a day in the summer holidays, almost every day, missing my kids and half killing myself so he could come home from hospital was *messing about.*

To date, everything he's accused me of throwing out has reappeared, apart from the record player which had the unfortunate accident with my foot. He still had to have a little whinge about a plastic egg timer.

Where did I put that big stick?

# Chapter 37

We were finally given the broadcast date for the hoarding programme. Imelda would be watching, with any luck with his new hearing aid installed, although perhaps it'd be better if he didn't hear some parts.

I was there for most of the time they were filming him and I monitored them all the time so that I could translate for him ~ and I wanted to make sure he didn't make himself look stupid.

When they were filming me though, he left us alone and let them get on with it while he pottered around the house.

We wouldn't be able to see the programme before it was transmitted. This made me somewhat nervous as if there had been anything awful which had slipped in, there was absolutely nothing I could have done about it. I knew programmes could be edited to make things appear to be different from reality, but I'd been assured that they wouldn't do this. They'd spoken to me having themselves seen the final cut and reassured me that everyone came across very well and that I had managed to show a caring side ~ although where they found that I'll never know.

I guessed Imelda would come across as a "sweet old gentleman". He has that knack.

People often said to me, "Isn't your father a lovely man?" Yes, he *can* be a right old charmer when he wants to be, but don't be fooled!

I was still concerned that I might come over as the total opposite ~ a right bossy old cow. I only hoped I'd be given the benefit of the doubt. I'd *had* to be forceful ~ the house had to be cleared or he wouldn't have been able to come out of hospital. I hoped that had been made clear. Even though Imelda just couldn't see a problem ~ and he still can't.

If I hadn't cleared the house he would've had to go into a residential home which would have been the worst option for all concerned. He's always been the independent sort and as soon as independence is removed from those over a certain age, they can go downhill fast.

I had four weeks until the airing date for the programme, during which time I intended to ensure I had a safe spot ready behind the sofa and a nice bottle of something medicinal in the cupboard. I thought about booking myself a little holiday straight afterwards.

I once saw an episode of the US show *Hoarders* and noticed the two hoarders featured could communicate with the interviewer totally normally, calmly and rationally about their individual hoards. Totally normal looking and sounding people you wouldn't look twice at in the street. I didn't expect them to have two heads, but I'd imagined the typical hoarder to look a bit scruffy and unkempt and rough around the edges. Not these hoarders: they looked entirely normal, and were smartly dressed with no hint of the chaos in which they lived.

These hoarders admitted they had a problem, and they'd like it to be dealt with. They accepted help from the TV show to help them de-clutter. Both of their houses were hoarded beyond belief, there was evidence of rodents in both properties and neither of the hoarders was able to sleep in their own bed.

Imagine relinquishing your precious bed to junk. You'd think as soon as it got that bad you'd stop! How could anyone get a proper night's sleep on a sofa?

One of the hoarders was about to be evicted if he didn't deal with the issue. Although these poor people's quality of life had deteriorated to the extent that their bathrooms and bedrooms were unusable for the purposes intended, they were still collecting.

The families of all the hoarders on the programmes evidently loved their hoarding relative and wanted to help. The hoarder was able to blank out the problem until confronted by other people in their house throwing out their stuff. They were OK for a while and then *crack.*

They all did it. Their sweet and charming outer facades crumbled as if they'd been holding back from showing emotion. Then, suddenly, they couldn't hold back ~ and they cracked, big time. There was anger, there were tears and there were full-on strops.

All of them said they couldn't deal with this "right now" ~ the very time they had willing helpers, psychiatrists, families and bin-lorries and the most ideal time to deal with it. They all displayed totally disproportionate anger at those trying to help. One accused her daughter of interfering when she really wasn't. The other was being frustratingly stubborn about keeping stuff in vermin-chewed boxes and was unable to explain why he wanted to keep these items; he got angry and frustrated and put his foot down about throwing stuff out.

Imelda did that. I'd tried the calm and rational approach with him. I tried to go through his items one by one. We'd chat about the item, we'd agree it could *probably* go out and we'd get as far as the 'I already have many of these and this one is an old and broken one. Out of all the ones I have in the house this one is in the worst condition and the oldest and so this is the most likely to be able to go out' pile.

Instead of making a decision, Imelda would take the thing from me and put it aside for later, then he'd put it on a different pile where it would remain.

Imelda's case was slightly different as the hoarders on this programme had either asked for help or had been persuaded to accept it for their own health and wellbeing by family members. Imelda had *never* asked for help, nor had he ever admitted he had a problem!

From my observations the hoarders themselves displayed similar hoarding and personality traits. It was good to know I wasn't alone. I could really feel for the families trying to help.

Imelda and I were also asked to appear on daytime television's *"This Morning"* programme on the same day the hoarding programme was to be aired.

Imelda was happy to agree to the show because he said he wanted to help people. Bless him! The fact he'd get a whole meal in the hotel the night before and a free breakfast didn't figure at all in his calculations. No, really!

I asked my friends and family on a social media site what they thought about us doing the live breakfast show and all my friends, without exception were very enthusiastic about it. Some of my family were extremely cautious though and tried to talk me out of it ~ however, I knew they'd support me either way. I think their cautiousness was because they knew Imelda whereas my friends didn't. My family knew he could be manipulative ~ and that he'd be in his element and on form with his charming old gentleman act. I listened to their concerns but decided to ignore them anyway. I knew my own mind and was sure I'd be OK.

I was quite excited about it and was looking forward to the whole experience. Surprisingly, Imelda was thrilled when he saw his picture in the TV magazine. Rather than being ashamed and embarrassed, he told everyone he had ever met that the programme was on ~ all the neighbours, his travel agent, the Vicar, his cousin in England whom he only hears from at Christmas, the postman, everyone in his church and the cashier in Tesco's. He clearly was very proud of himself.

I put the details of the programme on the hoarder forum ~ others on the forum thought he was extremely brave to be going public. They all said, without exception that they would have died of shame had anyone known about their hoarding and none of them would have been "brave" enough to have it put on the television. I think Imelda is too thick skinned for the notion of shame to even occur to him. He rang me and read out a list of at least twenty people he had called to tell them to watch him ~ he wanted to know if he'd left anybody out.

I asked him why he was telling everyone about the programme ~ if it were me I'd keep very, very quiet. His response was, 'Well I have nothing to hide! Nothing to be ashamed of, is there?'

Personally, I'd treat it the same as appearing on the "*Embarrassing Bodies*" programme with a genital wart. And *that's n*ever going to happen ~ and for clarity, no, I do not have a genital wart!

Imelda was extremely chuffed with himself acting as if he'd been nominated for an Oscar or a lifetime achievement award.

I wasn't allowed to take the day off work, so in between being in London for the morning TV show and at home for the documentary I had to squeeze in a shift, too. It would be a big day! I might just have to go to the pub with the girls after the programme as well to wind down...

The evening before the programme we went to the station to catch the train to London. Imelda doesn't often get out of his little world, so I did all the organising. When we got to the station, I had to collect our tickets from the ticket machine. Imelda was fascinated by this process and watched me transfixed. We went to the ticket control and I gave him his ticket and showed him where to put the ticket to get through the barrier. He refused to listen to me and instead he showed his ticket to the guard, proudly announcing, 'I haven't been on a train in at least twenty years.'

The guard looked at him and smiled. 'There are no steam trains up there,' he said, with an amused grin. Imelda looked somewhat out of place among the busy commuters. It was somewhat of a Harry Potter moment. He looked very 'Old School' and very out of place in a modern city train station.

We took our seats on the 17:15 Cardiff to Paddington. I sat by the window and Imelda took the aisle seat. After a few minutes Imelda started shuffling uncomfortably. There were a group of about six very camp, very loud, young men sitting at the table in front of our seat, all being rather *in your face* and they got louder and louder.

At Newport station a few of them got up to leave the train. As soon as they'd walked past us, while they were still standing waiting to get off and in full earshot, Imelda said loudly, 'I'm glad they've gone ~ they were giving me funny looks!'

He didn't mean to be loud but he hadn't brought his new hearing aid and didn't know how loud he was talking. I cringed, knowing they were standing just behind us, but couldn't resist asking what kind of looks. Imelda paused a moment and then, just as loudly said, 'come hither looks.' Priceless!

The rest of them stayed on the train until Swindon and started blowing Imelda kisses whenever he looked at them; it was difficult for him *not* to look at them because his seat faced theirs!

Imelda told the ticket inspector and everybody else on the train that he hadn't been on a train for twenty years. I think he thought he'd get special treatment.

All things technological fox Imelda. He was fascinated by how I knew where to go for the car to the hotel and how I knew which car was ours (all texted to me just as we got to Paddington). He followed me like a sheep, in awe at everything.

After dinner, Imelda decided he'd like to go for a walk as he's a London boy at heart. By this time it was about 11pm. I wasn't at all sure this was a good idea, but letting him out on his own wasn't a good plan either ~ an old man wearing a back brace was a sure target for any passing unsavoury element of society, especially late at night in London. I decided I'd go with him as long as he wasn't planning on walking far, but whether I was protecting him or he was protecting me wasn't clear.

We walked from the hotel towards Waterloo Bridge and then onto the bridge where we saw all the London landmarks lit up with their lights reflecting off the Thames. The moon was huge, full and bright that night; with the right company it could have been quite romantic.

Imelda decided we should go for a walk up the side of the Thames. It was midnight by this time and I didn't intend to leave him there on his own, nor was I going to walk back to the hotel alone, there being a fair few dodgy-looking geezers down by the river. I had visions of us being mugged and murdered. I put my handbag under my coat and tried to look streetwise, which wasn't easy under the circumstances! We walked along the river to see the ITV studios where the morning live programme would be broadcast from, before finally making it safely back to the hotel shortly after midnight.

# Chapter 38

We went to breakfast in the morning despite my stomach feeling like a butterfly breeding programme, and I managed a few croissants while Imelda ate a hearty breakfast as if he hadn't eaten in weeks.

On the way back to the room after breakfast we were in a very small lift with a skinny bloke aged about forty with facial stubble and tattoos on his forehead. He wore a cagoule with the hood up, a pair of pink tights and a tight, flowery skirt. He got off on the floor before us. I smiled politely at him as he got out. Imelda said in his not too quiet voice 'He was wearing a *skirt!*' I was starting to wonder if he would make it to the television studios with his remaining teeth intact.

At 9am we arrived at the television studios overlooking the Thames. We went through security and were directed up to the area where *This Morning* is filmed. I was asked by almost everyone if I was nervous. Oddly enough by now I wasn't and neither was Imelda. Imelda was hell-bent on eating all the freebies and asking for a tour of the studios.

I was taken to the make-up room and given a make-over. It was pretty weird to be sitting in a room no larger than my bathroom at home, in front of a mirror, surrounded by people I normally see the other side of the TV screen.

They made me look presentable and I went back to the Green Room. The main presenter came in to meet us before the airing and Imelda talked to him about way back in the BBC when they'd first met. They did seem to remember each other.

They miked us up and took us through all the small rooms to the studio where they film the show. We were asked to sit on the sofa, told where and how to sit, then 3-2-1 ~ and we were live on air!

It was just like sitting on a sofa chatting to my mates ~ except I kept telling myself not to slouch, shoulders back, check ear was not poking through my hair, check skirt not tucked in knickers ~ no, I was wearing trousers, cross ankles in a ladylike manner, check. I tried to say all I had to say clearly and slowly, using eye contact and everything else.

The presenter said Imelda was a well-dressed individual and a very "dapper" man, but then, he evidently hadn't noticed the baked bean stain on his shirt. Imelda had his brace on under his jacket which was, I believe, for the sympathy vote because he didn't need to wear it all the time any more.

They asked Imelda about the hoarding issue and whether he thought it was a problem. He said if he was honest he was aware there was a problem and knew he should do something about it but there was so much else to do. He said the garden was of course his priority as everybody could see it. This was after the images of the innards of his house had been spewed all over the television screens.

He deftly deflected the question about what he thought of the house after all my efforts desperately trying to clear it while he was in hospital. He was asked why he wouldn't throw stuff out. He waffled on about how the televisions were history and so he couldn't throw them away. That might explain the nine televisions ~ but what about the rest of the stuff?

The presenter said they'd have to finish the interview as they needed the sofa for the next guest and they could not take the risk of him covering it with stuff. Ha ha. At the end of the interview we chatted for a short while with the two presenters who were lovely and also appeared to be interested in the subject of hoarding. We had a photo taken and then had to leave to make way for the next guest.

Imelda had his brief tour of the studios before we were whisked off to Paddington station.

When we got to Paddington we got out of the car provided for us by ITV and noticed two people staring at us. They came up to us and said 'Oh, my goodness! We just watched you on the telly'. It was absolutely hilarious; Imelda was somewhat bemused as they asked for his autograph. He chuckled all the way home.

The train arrived at Cardiff central train station at 15:22 and the Welsh weather was hell bent on ruining my hair. I had to run from the train station to the bus station which wasn't far but I had no hood or brolly and my hair was looking the best it had looked in ages thanks to the ladies in make-up. I didn't want to ruin it.

I had to battle my way straight to work and was an hour late. As soon as I got into the office I noticed I was getting some strange looks and some people were staring at me. The office is huge, and I probably only know about 50 of the 500 or so people who work there. Apparently they'd had the programme on in the break area and one of the people I knew had seen it and pointed me out to the others. I was told there'd been a bit of a crowd gathered in there.

Throughout the day people came up to me and said "I saw you on the telly". I wasn't sure how to react. Any notions I had of staying anonymous went straight out of the window ~ and there was still the documentary to follow that evening.

After work I had thirty minutes to get home before the documentary started. I needed a stiff vodka and a cushion behind the sofa in case it all got a bit scary. I'd be watching it for the first time ~ along with millions of other people.

The programme started with Imelda, then on to an old lady in Florida who was *far* worse in that she had lost the use of her plumbing and resorted to "going to the bathroom" in plastic bags which she left on the kitchen floor. Her story was very sad ~ she'd even had to sleep on just one corner of her bed as it was covered in stuff. She also had an infestation of cockroaches which were everywhere and had managed to set fire to her kitchen as well. The smell in a small house in Florida with no air conditioning must have been horrendous.

Of the cases shown I was grateful to see Imelda's house was not the worst. I was less grateful to notice I had far more wrinkles that I realised ~ perhaps working at Imelda's house had aged me.

The programme showed me getting frustrated with him and him stubbornly refusing to throw *anything* out including the small square of disintegrating foam rubber with the clear indentation of a shoe in it.

I heard myself asking why he needed *eight* televisions in his living room ~ he'd said, 'Because I do'. We found the ninth in there the next day. He was shown clearly becoming frustrated and uncomfortable with the clear up process and also refusing to let me throw anything away.

For the record (just to show I'm not the daughter from Hell) the things I threw away on the day without running them past him first were such things as an ancient, stained pillow that the dog (that died three years before ~ the current dog has a different one) used to sleep on; a box of Lidl magazines; five year old holiday brochures; a box from a toaster many years old; a toaster corpse without the insides; a broken plug; a disintegrating slipper sole; a belt without the buckle; an old ice cream container with a hole in it; used Brillo pads ~ you get the idea!

On the whole I was pleased with the programme, which managed to get the frustrations of hoarding from both the point of view of the hoarders and their families. They managed to omit my inner axe murderess tendencies and they didn't make him look like a total idiot ~ or me a total bitch!

On the plus side (for me) they managed to catch his temper and frustratingly stubborn refusal to let me deal with anything. When I asked him why he wouldn't let me get rid of anything he actually said it was because he didn't trust me.

Imelda was recognised a few times around town after the programme. Even one of the men digging up the end of his road said, 'Oi mate! Weren't you on the telly the other day?' The bus driver recognised him and he had a few comments from strangers. He seemed to be quite the local hero and he was revelling in it.

He acted as if he was the victim in a, "Look at me and this horrendous mess I have to live in ~ poor me!" kind of way. I thought he'd missed the point, somehow.

At church, people approached him with, 'Have you cleared up that mess yet Bryn?' He laughed about it, though a comment like that was neither helpful nor productive. I'd nagged him for forty or more years to tidy it up ~ did anyone really think a comment like that would change anything?

Others had been supportive, saying how brave he was to let the cameras into his life and admit to such a problem. They told him how difficult they thought it must be to live like that ~ and so many people told him that they knew people like that.

There must be millions of hoarders suffering varying degrees of living with too much stuff around. The difference is that the other people would do their utmost to hide it. Imelda flaunted it on national television and then sat back and enjoyed the attention. Almost a "give me sympathy, people, I have a terrible recognised medical condition" attitude that gave him an excuse to carry on hoarding.

In his own eyes, Imelda was now a famous hero and far too busy being one to do anything as mundane as tidying his house ~ which has, therefore, deteriorated further since the programme.

I should also mention that the programme showed the house *after* I'd spent six weeks clearing it!

As for me ~ well, a few people in work saw the programme during their break in the staff room despite my efforts to turn it to a different channel the night before. I got the odd sarcastic comment that I was far too famous to be able to work with them now. There was a bit of mickey taking, but life soon got back to normal again. Most people have been very kind about it and said I came across as extremely patient. A few of the ladies in work said they thought my dad was really sweet ~ he's always had that effect on the ladies. I can't believe how the film crew made me come across as a saint! The number of screaming matches I'd had with Imelda was unbelievable. Perhaps by the time they filmed I'd more or less given up.

Of course Imelda seemed to come across as a very sweet, kindly and well-spoken old gentleman. I knew he would. Oh, how the camera can lie!

Happily, none of my main concerns about doing the programme had happened. I was worried we might get comments from some elements of the community or that perhaps Ant would have suffered some abuse. I have totally no regrets at all about doing either the live show or the programme. It was all a great experience in itself and I don't think I would've done anything differently if I could turn the clocks back.

# Chapter 39

Last night Imelda rang me asking to borrow my husband over the weekend. I asked him what he was up to.

'Well, you see, you know I had those blue armchairs given to me a few years ago from the Joneses over the road?'

'Yeeesss Dad.' I said, trying to anticipate what the daft old goat was going to tell me this time.

'Well, the Joneses are moving away, you see and they have offered me the matching blue sofa to go with the chairs because they don't want to take it with them.'

'That's marvellous news Dad ~ now you can get rid of the green sofa.'

'Yes well anyway,' he said, evidently dismissing or applying selective deafness to what I'd just said ~ he still hasn't worked out how to use his hearing aid. 'There isn't room for two sofas in the living room...'

'Great Dad – the council can collect the old one for you."

'..so I want to put one in the bedroom upstairs until there's enough room for it in the living room. Alternatively of course it would be nice to have a sofa in the bedroom but I need someone to help me take it upstairs.'

*Surely*, I thought, *he couldn't possibly be referring to the same living room and bedroom that I spent my whole summer clearing so he could have space to live. The same rooms featured on television being cleared and then being re-filled with all the junk and, and...*

Oh Dear God, NO! It was foot down time.

I said, 'Dad, no way. No way is that *ever* going to happen, sunshine! No, No, No, No, No, No, No and No. Either the old one goes or the new one isn't coming in. There is no way you are going to put that thing upstairs. No ~ the floorboards won't take it for starters and Neil is *absolutely not* going to put his back out humping that thing up the stairs. No Dad – No way!'

I was envisaging getting the green sofa through the house and up the stairs which were now totally re-cluttered. There was absolutely no way I was going to allow that to happen. I'd spent ten weeks or so breaking my back, ruining my lungs, and losing blood, sweat and tears over clearing his bedroom to make it half decent. Finally it now contained about half the junk it did then ~ and he wanted to put a scabby sofa in there. I voiced my opinion ~ it wasn't pretty.

'Oh NO!' he said, as if I'd got it all wrong, 'I know we won't get the green sofa up the stairs! Ha ha! We probably won't even get it out of the lounge at the moment.' I hadn't seen the house for about three weeks; heaven only knows what state it was in. Phew! Perhaps I'd misjudged him or misheard him. Silly me!

'No!' he said, 'I want to put the *blue* sofa upstairs until there's room to put it in the living room,' and then as if by way of an explanation 'It will go with the two chairs in the living room, you see.'

Call me naive but possibly he hadn't thought of the obvious. I thought I should at least suggest it. 'Dad, why don't you just *throw the old one out?*'

There was a long silence. 'Yeeessssss,' he said, as if just considering it as a remote possibility ~ or at least as if to *appear* that he was at least thinking about it to humour me. 'But that part is neither here nor there at the moment ~ the point is they want to get rid of it by next weekend.'

He'll never change!

# Chapter 40

It's now six months since the programme was filmed and two months since it was aired for the first time. Imelda is happily living at home with Ant and his back is healing well. The doctors believe his fall was due to a change in medication which had made his blood pressure very low and caused him to have dizzy spells including the one he had at the top of the ladder. It was perhaps a good thing he passed out at the top because if he'd been conscious as he fell he would have braced himself for the landing and probably broken more bones ~ the outcome could have been far worse.

Although I hesitate to use the word 'fortunate' under the circumstances, he was fortunate to have landed on grass and fortunate that he wasn't up a tree twice the height over a concrete path which is where he had been only an hour earlier. I've warned him I won't be happy if I find he's been climbing ladders again. Not that it will make a blind bit of difference.

He's sorted *one* of the three bags left by the clearance team; the other two are still on the sofa. The clutter has crept back up the stairs and over the bedroom floor. The kitchen table is hidden once again. The garden remains immaculate and the bins are still full of wood.

Imelda still calls me late at night asking where I put something which he can't find. Nothing much has changed. I don't think it ever will. If he is happy living there then who am I to tell him how to live? I'm close by if he needs me but apart from that I am leaving his house well alone. I've done my bit.

I still have my Mum's diaries safe in my own house. I've read every word on every page. I now have more of an insight through them of what kind of a person she was and of her thoughts. I know she loved Ant and me very much and she did her utmost for us despite the physical difficulties she had in the house. Reading between the lines I can see how Mum struggled with the growing hoard and the very stubborn hoarder.

I can't say for sure whether she had Alzheimer's disease or a mental breakdown. I'm not a medical professional. I do know that I would never be able to live in a house like that ever again, the effects it had on my physical health was bad enough. I don't know if it affected my mental health or whether I got out in time.

Imelda is 83 now and I've accepted I'll never change him so I've stopped trying. He's told me he 'probably' won't be going up the ladder again although he's eager to point out that now his medication has been changed he no longer has dizzy spells.

I've offered Imelda my help and told him to call if he needs me. My next task is to go round to dismantle the old green sofa. He accepted it had to go out and had it put in his garden to await its fate. I noticed he kept the sofa seat cushions and the wheels from underneath!

~

As I finish this book, ten months after the fall, Imelda's house is filling up again, the bins are still full of wood, none of the TV's have been fixed and he still hasn't found his socks. One of the bags is *still* on the sofa from the clear out day, the large TV from the neighbour's garage still doesn't work but remains, together with the other eight television sets, in his living room. Its stand remains in the middle of the floor – too heavy to move. The carpet on the stairs has still not been replaced and the kids still don't like visiting the house.

On the up side, Imelda's back is a lot better and he tells me he has not been up a ladder since.

# Thank You

Thank you for reading this book. Whether you read it because you live with a hoarder, know a hoarder or are a hoarder, I really hope you enjoyed it. It was my intention to just tell my story as I see it and not to judge. Every single hoarder and their situation is different and each should be approached differently. There are many web sites and social media pages dedicated to supporting both those who hoard and those who live with them - these sites have given me much support and encouragement and helped me realise there are many more people out there affected by hoarding. It helps just to know you are not alone.

**If you have enjoyed this book I would be extremely grateful if you could leave a review for it online. Every single review counts and I read each and every one. Should you wish to contact me personally you can do this through my Facebook page or my blog www.hevsblogs.blogspot.com. I would love to hear from you. You will also find photos of the house mentioned in this book on the blog and regular updates. Many thanks.**

# About the Author

Izabelle Winter lives in Cardiff, UK with her three children, partner and three pet snakes. Following the events leading to the writing of the book she is now happy to take a few months out to sit quietly at home eating Galaxy Bites and drinking beer.

When she's not clearing 'that house', she works as a Customer Service Manager for a retail company. When time permits she also loves skiing, sewing, carpentry, reading, photography, acting and getting out on her Kawasaki EN500 motorbike.

Over recent months she is happy to report she has been able to keep her 'mad axe murderer' tendencies under control and her psychiatrist reports she is doing well.

Imelda is continuing to recover from his fall. He has re-hoarded the house almost to its original state, re-filled the wheelie bins with wood and bought more shoes.

Printed in Great Britain
by Amazon